How to
speak with power

How to
speak

McGRAW-HILL BOOK COMPANY, INC.

STEPHEN S. PRICE

with power

New York   Toronto   London

HOW TO SPEAK WITH POWER

Library of Congress Catalog Card Number: 59-15304

FIRST EDITION

To my wife Inge
with love

THIS BOOK CAN HELP YOU

In Personal Relations

Express yourself clearly and easily

Speak with confidence and poise in all your dealings with people

Develop the positive voice qualities that people like to remember

Give your conversation a lift—make it more interesting and entertaining

Gain more attention and appreciation from family and friends

Attract interesting friends wherever you go

In Business Relations

Sell yourself and your ideas

Achieve more respect and prestige in your business or professional dealings

Gain cooperation more easily and quickly in getting the job done

Win recognition and the rewards of leadership by persuasive speaking

Speak with ease and influence to large and small groups

In Everyday Living

Participate in new and interesting activities

Create true understanding and warm appreciation in love and marriage

Widen your horizons for richer and happier living

CONTENTS

Contents

PART SIX   SPEAK IN PUBLIC WITH
                 NEW CONFIDENCE

Part One

PUT YOUR BEST VOICE FORWARD

Chapter One

YOUR VOICE REVEALS
WHAT YOU ARE

Every day in every way your voice reveals what you think —how you feel—what you do. But does your voice persuade or irritate—attract or repel?

Does your voice say the same thing as your words? Although words and voice usually "agree," in some cases the words speak one language, the voice another. When the word is "Yes" but the voice tone says "Maybe," which do you believe? As you listen closely to people you'll find it's the voice that more often tells the truth.

I wouldn't think of asking you to become a voice detective, but it is important to open your eyes—and your ears —to the deeper symbols of human relations revealed in the voice. After all, voice tones were the only "language" for thousands of years—long before words were invented.

Your voice, as unique as your fingerprints, can be recognized in the dark or on the phone. People unconsciously index you in their minds by the sound of your voice.

The best way to hear your voice as others hear it is to record your voice. But if you can't, just step close to the corner of a room, face the corner, cup your ears—then count or say words in your usual voice. That strange-sounding voice you hear is really yours.

When you listen to the first playback of your recorded voice, you may not even recognize it. Because our speaking and hearing organs are so closely connected, we cannot hear ourselves as others hear us. The voice is like a camera in the sense that a camera cannot take a picture of itself.

The voice you hear is the voice that others know you by, the voice that has been labeling you in people's minds. Every time you meet someone at a party . . . or chat with a casual acquaintance . . . or greet a customer . . . or speak at a club meeting, the opinions people form about you are influenced by your voice.

Whole industries are "voice-conscious." To name one, the airline passenger service has been aware since its inception that its personnel can give passengers a feeling of confidence—or of anxiety. The tone of voice is important—not only in the air, but also at the reservation desk.

Airline stewardesses spend many hours recording their voices on tape and listening to playbacks—their one purpose: to give their voices warmth and assurance. Pursers are chosen especially for their firm, cheerful voices. Airline pilots must frequently speak to passengers over the intercom—and an assured, pleasant voice does much to create confidence.

Whatever is said by military flying personnel, cruise-car policemen and firehouse dispatchers, clarity of speech is essential. The degree of clarity with which an airman shouts "MIG at 4 o'clock" during a sky battle can determine life and death. During World War II I helped Air Force pilots learn to enunciate clearly. One warm-up phrase I used to ask them to shout in unison: "Tea, tea. The boys will have some tea!" put real vigor into their voices.

Have you hopes of climbing the "executive ladder"? If so, you can't afford to overlook the benefits of a good speaking voice. When an acquaintance of mine—in line for a vice-presidency of his firm—was passed over, I asked an executive who knew about this what had happened. He explained, "Joe missed out because—we-l-l, to be frank, he doesn't *sound* like a vice-president. Joe has such a thin, uncertain voice that the boss was afraid he might make important customers lose confidence in us." I might add that Joe is now working to put more assurance into his voice.

Whether you are an executive, doctor, lawyer, secretary, salesman . . . whether you are a white-collar worker or wear overalls—your voice is important in your day-to-day living. In our world—largely a "speaking world"—your voice represents you, just as the salesman represents his product.

The president of a pharmaceutical house, in making arrangements for me to analyze and fortify the sales pitch of his salesmen, explained, "Competition in our market is really rough. I've watched good items go down the drain 'cause they weren't sold right. The answer has to be sales. We've got a lot of incentive campaigns, but I keep after the boys to 'beef up' the sales pitch. I want my boys to really sell!"

Do you sell when your voice speaks for your product— or service? Are your abilities well represented by your voice in your "market"—whatever it may be? Does your voice help or hinder when you try to express warmth—authority —confidence?

The wealthy owner of four radio stations in different states told me flatly about his money-making policy. "I cut my overhead down to the bone . . . but my announcers get the best pay in town. I search high and low for the friendly, respected type of voice. My announcers don't *represent*—they *are*—my station. You might say people tune us in to have a friend in the house."

What qualities do you "broadcast" in your voice? Most

people don't have to be psychologists to figure out how you feel—they can hear it in your voice.

The lists of personality characteristics used by two companies in rating employees for hiring, promotions or dismissal appear below. Would it surprise you to learn that most of these characteristics are expressed by the voice?

From the personnel file of Remington Rand:

Desirable	Undesirable
Enthusiastic	Tactless
Sincere	Argumentative
Tactful	Diffident
Confident	Sullen
Sociable	Obstinate
Cheerful	Conceited
Determined	Sarcastic

From the personnel file of The Hoover Company:

Positive	Negative
Alert	Nervous
Cheerful	Moody
Enthusiastic	Pessimistic
Modest	Sarcastic
Patient	Intolerant
Sympathetic	Suspicious
Self-reliant	Jealous
Optimistic	Bossy
Considerate	Egotistical
Understanding	Boastful
	Arrogant
	Shy
	Dependent

Your voice reveals negative, as well as positive, attitudes, moods and reactions. For example:

What you think of yourself
When you become excited
When you are frustrated
When you get angry
When you are worried
When you are nervous
When you are suspicious
When your feelings are hurt
When you are unsure of yourself
When you are discouraged
When you are self-conscious, shy, timid, inhibited, afraid

Some of the positive voice tones are: warmth, enthusiasm, authority, energy, sympathy, sincerity, cheerfulness.

Really listen to others and pay special attention to the way they speak. Yes, I know, all your life you've been hearing, "It's not *what* you say—it's *how* you say it." But when you really tune in, you'll be able to hear what people mean as well as what they're saying. You should then be able to spot the many different meanings of "ah-a-a," "what," or "yes." It all depends on who says it, where, to whom and how.

How many different things can people mean when they say "Yes"? Let's look at only a few:

The Word	The Meaning
"Yes"	Of course . . .
"Yes"	No!
"Yes"	Well . . . maybe.
"Yes"	Really? I don't believe it.
"Yes"	Now are you satisfied?
"Yes"	I'm not sure.
"Yes"	. . . and what are you going to do about it?
"Yes"	. . . now leave me alone!
"Yes"	Oh! What an idiot you are!
"Yes"	Will . . . this . . . never . . . end!

One of my very recent assignments was to evaluate customer relations of key employees of a giant New York department store—in terms of their speaking ability. Special attention was given to "return" and credit personnel, switchboard operators and various executives. I talked with each by phone and with some in person, sometimes as a problem customer. A few did poorly in the "stress" tests—their impatience and irritation came through in their attitudes and voices. Reports indicate that the trouble-shooting course we worked out for key employees did much to improve customer relations.

Another large department store, this one in the Midwest, made a survey of customers in an attempt to rate the "popularity" of its clerks. Nine out of ten of the men and women who rated high in popularity were found to have improved their voices by singing—in school glee clubs or church choirs—or by acting in amateur plays. Since its survey, this store has paid particular attention to the voices of job applicants.

Perhaps one of the greatest tests of all for the voice is romance. More than one woman has confided to me that it was the warmth and assurance in her husband's voice that first intrigued her.

A teen-age boy puts his voice to a test whenever he tries to sell a popular girl on the idea of a date. And we all have heard the beauty who weakens her appeal by nagging voice tones.

Women, even more than men, instinctively listen to the feeling behind words. If "I love you, darling" isn't said convincingly, the words sound as hollow as a dead tree trunk. If you have a pet dog, you may almost feel that he understands every word, but I'm sure you know it's the sounds that make sense to him. Words by themselves are as "empty" to him as clean plates. You might like to try this "voice versus words" experiment:

Talk to him in warm, affectionate tones, but say such words as, "You bad, bad dog . . . come here and I will beat the daylights out of you." Then watch him come to you wagging his tail. Later, try the other half of the experiment. Using the kind of words that usually make his tail wag with joy, speak in a loud, angry voice, saying such words as: "You are the nicest doggy . . . here's a juicy bone for you."

Harold East, a Hollywood trainer who has taught dogs everything from horseback riding to dancing, emphasizes: "The big control in all dog training is tone of voice. Admonish the dog sternly when he misbehaves. Praise enthusiastically all good behavior."

As you listen for certain clues in the tone and color of the voice, how do you react? Notice how high-pitched, loud or gruff voices will annoy and irritate you. But also notice how warm, friendly voices in the lower tones—not too soft or loud—will attract you.

Some years ago, as a CBS radio-TV director, I would single out men and women from studio audiences to participate in quiz and interview shows. I would chat with each one for a few minutes to size up personality-voice qualities. Out of twenty I would be lucky to find one who had a pleasant voice. Six might rate fair, but the voices of the majority would have caused our listeners to feel uncomfortable and possibly tune us out.

Detectives and secret-service men always listen for clues not only in words but also in voices. Michael McDougall, the world-famous authority on gambling, often called in by police departments and the F.B.I., told me while I was helping him prepare for his broadcasting: "In all my work in nabbing gambling cheats, every clue counts. I've broken cases because the tone of voice of a criminal tipped me off that he was lying." He added, "I've also talked my way out of many tough spots by speaking slowly in a calm voice.

Do I carry a gun? If I did, I'd have been dead a long time ago."

Like music and color, the voice speaks a universal language. If you've ever talked to someone whose words are unintelligible—perhaps a person who doesn't speak English or speaks it with a heavy accent—his gestures and facial expression may have helped you to understand him, but most of your understanding probably came from the feelings revealed by his voice.

I was called in by the Office of War Information, soon after the United States entered World War II, to supervise and direct special news and drama programs for broadcast around the clock to European countries. One of my first assignments was a series of dramatizations in Turkish. Because the Turkish programs were based on translations from English scripts, I developed a system of marking the English and Turkish scripts that made it possible for me to follow both continuously.

I recall the first rehearsal of this program because it dramatically points up the "language" of the voice. Stopping an actor while he was delivering a phrase that I felt deserved greater feeling, I asked him to try it again. The phrase was "Seni seviyorum sekerim." (I love you, my sweet.) Perplexed, the actor stared at me, no doubt wondering how I had the nerve to direct him in a language that I could not speak. All he'd expected was for me to time the program. The others in the studio exchanged a few words and then turned to stare at me. After asking the actor to read the line again, I mimicked his pronunciation—but added the tender tones I wanted him to use. Everyone looked surprised, and the actor said seriously, "That is perfect Turkish. You must *know* our language."

The Turkish broadcasts were a success, and all went well with one exception. I found that very little Turkish was spoken whenever I was around. Word had got around that

I knew more Turkish than I would admit to, and the more I denied it, the more the Turkish actors thought I was playing a joke on them.

People often ask, "How long is it going to take me to develop my voice and speak better? Since progress always depends on the individual, no one can really say how long it will take. But experience shows that people who feel they want to do something about their voices make surprisingly rapid improvement. If your voice is weak, you can make it more powerful; if you feel it sounds monotonous, you can make it more colorful; and if you want to overcome a harsh quality, there are ways to soften the tones.

In the following chapters you will find new and practical techniques to help you make your voice more pleasant, more powerful and more interesting. And everyone who really wants to can make his voice more appealing and develop a more winning speaking personality.

Chapter Two

MAKING THE WEAK
VOICE MORE POWERFUL

During a rehearsal of a Broadway play, the director was particularly worried about one actor. "I can't *hear* you, George! And if *I* can't hear you, the *audience* won't be able to hear you." "But," complained the actor, "if I shout, I'll lose the naturalness of my character." "Sure, and if the audience can't *hear* you," sighed the director, "you might as well not come on stage."

Lack of voice power to put over what you're saying is just as important in everyday life as on stage. In many professions—selling, for instance—voice power can make the difference between failure and success.

Since things were not working out for a chemical engineer whose company had promoted him to be a sales representative, he was sent to me for help. We talked briefly and then recorded his "sales pitch." After listening to the playback, I asked for his reaction. Thinking for a moment, he said, "I don't know what it is, but I guess it doesn't sell me." We agreed that his sales talk did make a poor impression—mainly because his voice was too weak. "But I know my product thoroughly," he explained, "and I can talk about it for hours. I just can't understand why my voice should be so important."

"Do you agree," I asked, "that selling is persuading?" He nodded. "Then you might say that trying to sell with a weak voice is like dropping a petunia down the Grand Canyon and listening for the echo." His understanding chuckle told me he was ready to start.

A weak voice is the result of insufficient breath power; breath power is needed first to vibrate the vocal cords, second to help form the sounds and finally to be amplified through resonance. Effective speaking begins with breath control.

Since a weak voice, which goes hand in hand with poor articulation, is frequently not understood, it gives a poor personal impression. It can be thin, breathy, wispy, unsure or a "little voice."

People who have weak voices explain their difficulties in statements such as these:

"People lean over to me as if they're hard of hearing."
"They keep asking me what I said."
"I'm so nervous when I talk because I think people don't understand me."
"When I tell anyone my ideas, they don't pay much attention. Everybody treats me like a baby."

Since those whose voices are weak are not always heard or clearly understood, they may become tense and frustrated, which further interferes with breathing coordination.

If people don't pay much attention to you or frequently ask you to repeat what you've said, you may have difficulty in persuading them, because a weak voice reveals lack of confidence. If you feel shy, unsure of yourself, or are usually tired, uncertainty or fatigue will be heard in your voice. Also, if you have little reserve energy, you will get tired quickly while talking.

The source of a weak voice can sometimes be traced to

childhood experiences. Dr. George A. Dorsey's dramatic statement makes clear the extreme effect on the voice that such experiences can have.

"Give me a newborn child, and in ten years I can have him so scared he'll never dare to lift his voice above a whisper, or so brave that he'll fear nothing."

One day a restaurant owner complained in his thin voice that he didn't mind if others overlooked him, but he couldn't stand his wife not listening. All his speech sounds seemed to form in the front of his mouth, giving an impression of "littleness." I asked this friendly but timid man if his employees listened to him. His reply: "Well, yes, because if they don't, I work up enough courage to fire them. But the chef, he's like my wife—he never listens to me. That's because I can't afford to let him go, and he knows it."

My first step was to reveal to him how powerful a voice he really had.

Walking about thirty feet away from him, I asked the restaurateur to project his voice to me. When he first tried, he couldn't make it. He then tried again, this time with a megaphone. (You can make one by rolling up a magazine or cardboard.) With the aid of the megaphone he was able to reach me with his voice. Then, standing only fifteen feet away, he tried again, this time with a little more confidence but without the megaphone. With a little extra effort he successfully projected his voice and was now ready to follow through with special exercises to secure his newly discovered voice power.

You may want to try the exercises which helped this restaurant owner speak more forcefully. He opened his mouth very wide—as if holding a bubble he didn't want to break. Next, he yawned several times to get the sensation of relaxing his throat. I asked him, first, to press his hands against his diaphragm (just above the midriff) for better breath support, and next, while "thinking and feeling *big*," to spread his feet apart, taking the pose of a strong man with clenched fists. From this position he projected the following sounds with controlled force:

> Boom—boom—boom
> Boomlay—boomlay—boom.
> Me Chief Big Bear. Me go now.
> You come show me. How!
> So—go—row.

Listening to his new voice encouraged him to continue the exercises at home, in this case his restaurant (after closing). To be sure he could project his new voice tones, he enlisted the help of a sympathetic busboy, who would listen to him from the other end of the empty restaurant.

Some of the open-sound phrases he practiced are:

> Oh boy, a pound of powder and potatoes.
> Pass the salt and pepper, please.
> Now go out to sweep and don't bend the big broom.

As a first step in building up his resonance, I advised him to cup his hands over his nose and mouth, then speak in a half-singing tone several words with nasal sounds (*n*, *m* and *ng*)—words like "ping," "ring" and "ming"—over and over, letting them ring out. Then he repeated these words, keeping a hand on his chest to feel the sympathetic resonance of the chest tones.

Before long he began to speak with more authority. As you'd expect, he first tried his "new voice" out on the chef. To his astonishment, the chef turned completely around, looked at his boss in surprise—and actually listened.

Weak voices are known to be more prevalent among women than men. The more important reasons have to do with shallow breathing, poor posture, constricted clothing and lack of energy. Some women, having mistaken ideas about femininity, don't open their mouths enough while talking. When energy is low and breathing shallow, the voice will sound breathy and thin.

Many movie starlets remain starlets because of their thin, "pussy-cat" voices. And some of the most beautiful women are disappointed in life because of their un- promising, inexpressive voices.

In the Miss America contests the finalists are given just one test of their charm—they are asked to talk briefly about themselves in front of a microphone. Even though many finalists were sensational in appearance, they cried their eyes out when their thin voices—lacking in per- sonality—quickly eliminated them. Future contenders for the Miss America title take note!

You would hardly believe the big changes that come over people after they have developed their voice power by proper exercise of the diaphragm. A woman now prominent in her North Carolina community made great progress in a short time. A shy, middle-aged person with a whispery voice, she had withdrawn from people after a tragic in- cident in her life. I learned that her hobby was cooking (she had once attended the famous Cordon Bleu cooking school in Paris). To get her into contact with people I persuaded her to accept an offer to teach a cooking course to young women at the YWCA. Learning how to speak with more energy and authority established her confidence, and she thoroughly enjoyed teaching cookery to her stu- dents. After a few months she became so busy with her many new friends that memories of her earlier problem all but disappeared.

Probably you have never given much thought to your diaphragm—that band of muscle a few inches above your midriff. Yet the diaphragm is your bellows—it blows the fire of life into your speech and adds the "oomph" to your personality. If your diaphragm is either lazy or weak, it will not give you enough breath support—an essential to good speaking.

A young research expert with a wispy, unsure voice complained, "When I talk in a group, I rarely get a chance to finish a sentence. Someone always butts in." He couldn't figure out why the girls he'd be talking with—even his dates —could always be diverted by other people's conversation.

Placing my hand on his diaphragm, I asked him to say loudly, "Boomlay, boomlay, boomlay, boom!" His frail diaphragm muscle barely fluttered. A well-developed diaphragm is firm and will really bounce whenever you say "boom."

We first worked to give him a feeling of more vigorous physical power. Boxing lessons and daily deep-breathing exercises helped increase his vitality. He learned about his diaphragm by stretching out on the floor, face up, and breathing deeply. After placing a heavy book on his diaphragm, he watched it rise and fall. (Try it yourself.) He would then shout several times "hay . . . hee . . . hah . . . hie . . . hoe . . . hoo," all the time keeping his hand on his diaphragm to feel its action.

Then, standing up, he did another exercise. Taking a deep breath, he would let his breath out slowly through pursed lips, as in whistling. Next, picking up a newspaper and taking a good breath, he would read aloud as long as that breath lasted. When he stopped, we would count the number of seconds his breath had lasted. As his diaphragm strengthened and his breath control improved, he could read for fifteen and, later, twenty seconds "on *one* breath." (Twenty-five is excellent!)

Meanwhile he learned to smile more often—to be the first to speak—to observe and sincerely compliment others. His self-assurance increased as we developed his conversational skill and joke-telling techniques.

As his voice grew stronger, he was no longer overwhelmed by others. When he was interrupted without good reason, he was able to recapture the spotlight merely by repeating the last phrase, but in a firmer voice. He had learned in a friendly way to command others.

When phoning recently to tell me about a young woman he had been dating, he announced happily, "Last year I figured she wouldn't even date me, but last night I persuaded her to marry me."

Breath control, not mere lung capacity, is what will make your voice outstanding. The long-held notes of Lily Pons, a petite person, are mainly the result of good diaphragm control. If a balloon filled with air represents lung capacity, then the gradual squeezing of the balloon to force the air out at the rate desired can be thought of as breath control. That's why many people who have lots of breath in their lungs do not necessarily have good breath control.

If you listen to people who have poor breath control, you will hear a lot of breath wasted and also many incomplete sounds that are not well produced.

In words containing the letters "p," "b," "t," "d," "v," "f," "w," and "h," breath is more easily wasted, especially if the word starts with any of these letters. The following sentence, designed to test your breath power, contains sounds (h, b, p, d, t) that cause breath to escape unused. The result is diffused sounds.

Read the following sentence aloud on *one* breath.

> He hid at home and sobbed when his sister
> seized whatever he had on top, in the thin,
> five-shelved closet.

If your breath control needs to be improved, you will find that you sound breathy and are out of breath by the time you reach the middle, or that your voice will fade toward the end and you will feel strained. Actually, a person with good breath control can repeat this phrase about four times on a *single* breath.

There's another way to test your breath control. Hold a lighted candle about four inches from your mouth, and, without blowing out the candle, say, "Peter Piper picked a peck of pickled peppers."

If the flame only flickers, that's fine. If you blow out the flame after every try, your breath control needs improvement.

Once you have strengthened your breath control and have the "feel" of a supported voice, you will speak with more power and authority.

Chapter Three

MAKING THE MONOTONOUS
VOICE COLORFUL

Many people are unfairly thought to be boring simply because their voices are monotonous. No matter what they
say, however interesting, it all sounds like a laundry list. No
doubt you've met people, even speakers at public meetings, whose tiresome monotones made you squirm.

If you think your voice is dull or monotonous, or if your
habitual speaking pace is like a "slow boat to China"—your
voice is probably creating a poor impression.

Look at people carefully while you talk to them. If they
seem bored or restless—if they fidget, cough or show other
signs of restlessness—your voice may be the cause.

People who lack zest for life usually lack voice color, too.
They are often phlegmatic, low in energy and spirit, and
their faces reflect little enthusiasm. Voices that are almost
completely lacking in color frequently reflect inhibitions or
repressions. The voice reflects all personality characteristics
more than is realized.

By contrast, the responsive voice is more flexible—more
interesting—more indicative of a responsive person. If your
voice does not mirror your thoughts and feelings, it limits
your ability to express yourself. But if you make some ef-

fort to put vitality in your voice, you will be happily surprised with the results.

Many men talk within a limited pitch range—perhaps only two or three tones—and with little change in tempo and volume. Others force their voices unnaturally to make them sound low-pitched and masculine. The result is a limited color range and harsh quality. The first step, therefore, is to locate the natural basic pitch—the "home-plate" pitch.

It sounds funny when a boy tries to imitate his dad's voice, forcing his lowest tones. It's sort of cute, too, when Mom, in reading to the children, imitates Baby Bear in her highest pitch. But if a person talked that way all the time, forcing his voice up into the "attic" or down into the "cellar," his voice would amuse some but irritate others. He is not using his voice comfortably, probably gets tired easily after talking a while, and his voice sounds harsh and monotonous. A good basic range, which begins with the "home-plate pitch," allows for easy variations in pitch without strain or discord.

In order to test whether you are using your best home-plate pitch tones, sing the scale. Go as high and then as low as you can without forcing. You can immediately tell where your voice is most comfortable. Piano accompaniment will help you locate your middle register notes, which should serve as the reference point for both the higher and lower tones.

You can locate your most natural pitch by another method, also. Gently put your forefingers into your ears to shut off outside sounds, and hum up and down the scale; listen especially for the notes that you hear yourself amplifying comfortably and with resonance. These notes are your main base or home-plate pitch.

A real-estate man, elected to an office in his club, asked me to help him increase his skill in managing meetings.

As a young man he had felt his voice sounded too high-pitched and had lowered his voice tones. But recently his wife had told him his voice was monotonously dull. A keen golfer, he had soon realized that a voice "locked" in low tones is as ineffective as playing golf with locked knees. In both, the strokes must be full, free, and balanced. You can check your voice range in the same way we checked his.

One way to test whether your voice is dull or interesting is to sing the scale up and down with the sound "la." Another test is to say "Why?" in five measured scale steps, starting at your lowest pitch and ending at your highest. Then, as you go up—then down—the scale several times, repeat "Now." If, as you go up and down the scale, your changes in pitch cannot be heard distinctly, your voice needs more color.

A prim New England woman who was to give a talk to the members of her women's club told me she was worried about how she would sound. Listening to her voice on a tape recorder, she realized how cold and listless her voice sounded. I asked her if she knew anyone who got a big kick out of life. She thought a moment and said, "Yes, the Italian handyman who helps with our gardening." She told me how much she admired his exuberance and joy of living.

Before she could bring warmth to her voice, she would have to learn to relax and become more responsive. One assignment was for her to spend a few hours each week working along with the handyman, planting shrubs and tending the large garden.

Other improvement sessions at home started with an exercise that would help her "let go." She would imitate a jolly Santa Claus by laughing "ho-ho-ho—ha-ha-ha—hee-hee-hee—hoo-hoo-hoo." If you want to try it, use the same laughing sounds. Start slowly, but as you go faster and faster, your sounds will turn into real laughter. After two months her voice took on more warmth of expression, and she began to get more fun out of life.

A balance of higher- and lower-pitched tones is needed for a complete "tone-contrast picture" and interesting expression. To avoid harshness in the higher-pitched tones, relax the throat and jaw.

Read aloud the excerpt given for pitch practice, repeating it several times, one paragraph at a time. To get the feel of it, make the pitch changes broad in your first run-through. Keep in mind your voice-pitch tendencies—if your pitch tends to be high, you may find that you go *too* high on high tones; if your pitch tends toward the low tones, it may be *too* low. By keeping your comfortable high and low tones in mind, you can counteract going too far in either direction while you work for tone balance and contrast.

What makes time pass slowly? What makes time pass quickly? Time—the time you feel by—is not measured by the clock on the wall. It is measured by the clock in your brain!

The clock in your brain is run by the way you feel. When it runs fast, minutes seem like hours. When it runs slow, it runs minutes into seconds.

Some people have inner clocks that always run slow. For them, it is always later than they think. They are always late in meeting people. For them, the clock on the wall goes too fast. They never catch up with it.

There are others whose inner clocks run too fast. For them time moves slowly. Fifteen minutes may seem like an hour. They are always early in meeting people.

"This Week"

Many voices are dull and uninteresting only because people don't know what to do about them. But remember that the person behind the voice can help by developing his expressive feelings.

The foundation of a colorful and interesting voice is built as the person begins to feel more deeply, become more sensitive to others, and reach out for new paths in living. Just releasing some of your inhibited feelings will give your voice freedom to come "from the heart"—not (as Robert Benchley put it) "from the roof of the mouth." The power of feeling in the voice was made clear by the all-time-great entertainer, Maurice Chevalier, in a *New York Times* interview when he said:

Any third-rate chanteur de charme [crooner] has a better voice than I. But they sing from the throat while I sing from the heart.

Chevalier declares that he's had little room in his life for gloom. His is a gay heart, and his singing has always reflected this.

Chevalier's artistry is based upon his ability to hold your attention. So are electric signs. Why does business invest so much money in electric signs? For this very purpose— to attract your attention. But how? By action with lights —continual change of the lights and the design. And the sign that flashes on and off may hold your attention for a second or two, but the one that makes more complex designs will hold your attention much longer. On the other hand, you may hardly notice a sign that is stationary.

"No one can possibly attend continuously to an object that does not change . . ." wrote psychologist William James. The same principle applies to sound as well as to sight.

In the world of music a thematic phrase may be played in seven seconds, but the variations (musical design) based on this theme are developed into a forty-minute symphony.

To begin making your voice more colorful and interesting:

- always be aware of variations in voice pitch and rhythm
- speak with greater intensity and voice power
- put more feeling into your voice—let yourself go

Most people who lack voice color have certain inhibitions which make them appear rigid. They need to relax and take things easier—with less tension. As Will Rogers used to remind an unyielding friend, "It's great to be great, but it's greater to be human."

Most of the exercises that follow should help you to inject more color into your voice. To stimulate the voice, we try first to free the body. The first step is to ignore any feelings of being silly or childish. Let me assure you that many a dignified businessman has learned to enjoy these "letting-loose" exercises.

The following exercise for pitch variation will quickly help you release any inhibitions you may have. Imitate the sound of a drum with your voice on different pitch levels. What kind of sound does a small parade drum make? "Prrrrrrrrrrrum-pat*um*, prrrrrrrrrrrum-pat*um*, prrrrrrrrrrrum-patupatuhp*um*tap*um*." First, take your highest pitch, then your lowest comfortable pitch, and follow with a medium one. Then let your voice go up and down, freely making broad changes in your pitch.

Make up some of your own rhythms. Think of a marching melody with a firm drum beat. It helps if you march—even in place—and pretend to beat on an imaginary drum. If you feel a little stiff, that's a sure sign you need limbering up. Just let go.

A dignified banker became so intrigued by this make-believe drumming that he bought a set of drums. And while he was drumming vitality into his voice he also had a relaxing hobby. Relaxing, that is, until his wife, who couldn't stand the noise, threatened to leave him. But

peace and harmony returned to the household after the
game room was soundproofed.

Another exercise that improves voice color and rhythm
is also one the banker enjoyed. Perhaps you will, too.
Simply play a recording of march music and march around
the room, singing with the music. You don't have to know
the lyrics—"pum-puh-rum-pum" will do (try imitating the
Dragnet theme).

If you're tired of marching, try conducting and sing to
the music (as Toscanini used to do). Put spirit into it and
really impersonate a conductor. Body freedom will help
voice freedom.

Another way to awaken your sense of pitch is to use a
little trick you may recall from childhood. Just wrap some
tissue paper around a comb and play yourself a little tune.

You may wish to try other techniques designed to release vocal inhibitions. For instance, try to be as dramatic
as Billy Graham. Practice broad, dramatic gestures.

Try the cheer leader's yells—the body action that goes
with these yells should help you really let go.

Sis, boom, bah!
Yay, team, team, team!

One effective exercise works very well on the stairs.
While you're walking downstairs, lower your voice pitch
with each step and say, "I'm now walking down, down,
down, down." Then, as you go up, make your sounds go
up, too: "I'm now climbing up, up, up." Coordinating your
body movements and voice will help you recognize and
control your pitch changes.

You can have a field day with voice color when reading
stories aloud to children. Animation and energy are a must
in children's stories. Imitate every sound—and make faces,
too. The small fry will love it, and the more exaggerated
your delivery the more they'll love it. Review the stories

beforehand to explore their possibilities, and make sure they have sound effects ("The train went 'choo-choo'"). Make up your own stories with sound effects.

Mojeska, the great Polish actress, gave us a supreme example of what a skilled voice can do when she visited the United States in the 1930s. Because she couldn't speak English, she delivered a monologue in Polish. Her American audience was deeply moved—some even wept. Her "monologue" was simply the Polish alphabet.

When you are ready to check on your voice improvement, tell a story like "The Three Bears" by using only numbers, giving each the inflection you would to the syllable it stands for. For example:

Once upon a time
1   2–3   4   5

There were three bears
6   7   8   9

Now that you know you can direct your pitch scale down to the cellar and up to the attic, the next step to a lively voice is to think, feel and gesture while your voice glides up and down the pitch scale.

Begin at your highest pitch and finish at your lowest. As you go up, lift your head slightly, looking up with your eyes; as your voice goes down, bring your head down slightly, looking down with your eyes. Moving your head, eyes, and voice in unison will help your pitch placement. Coordinate your voice and motion in the same rhythm.

Sigh while you say, "Oh, what's the use?" (First, glide downward, then reverse the process.)

Follow the same routine on these other phrases:

Now you tell me
If you wish
You know
Please

Now try combinations of two phrases:

start low and glide up	*start high and glide down*
Can't you go there?	Oh, I see.
Is it raining?	No, it's not.
Is the sun out?	I think it is.

Now reverse the above process:

start high and glide down	*start low and glide up*
Then we agree.	I don't know if we do.
She's waiting for you.	Waiting for me?
It doesn't make any difference.	Yes, it does.

With this bit of philosophy by Henrik Ibsen, practice the up-and-down glide. On (1) start at a low pitch and glide up to a high pitch—then on (2) glide down.

(1) Money may buy the husk of many things, (2) but not the kernel.
(1) It brings you food, (2) but not appetite
(1) Medicine (2) but not health
(1) Acquaintances (2) but not friends
(1) Servants (2) but not faithfulness
(1) Days of joy (2) but not days of happiness

Notice, however, how monotonous the repetition of a static up-and-down pattern can sound. Now try it again, and this time break up the rhythm and create different pitch variations while making the meaning clear and interesting.

A final reminder: When in doubt about your voice, try to get a burst of enthusiasm. It will add living color and vitality to your voice. As Robert Schauffler wrote in *The Atlantic Monthly:*

Enthusiasm is the thing that makes the world go round. Without its driving power, nothing worth doing has ever been done. It alleviates the pains of poverty and the boredom of riches.

Apart from it, joy cannot live. Therefore, it should be husbanded with zeal and spent with wisdom. To waste it is folly; to misuse it, disaster.

The lift of enthusiasm in your voice gives color and value to your words—the shadings and nuances that will help you gain the attention and respect of your listeners.

Chapter Four

MAKING THE HARSH
VOICE PLEASANT

If you ever have the feeling that people are uncomfortable when you talk, it may be that your harsh tones are hurting their eardrums. Your voice will sound unpleasant if it is shrill, grating, hard, piercing, brassy, too loud or nasal.

These harsh voice qualities usually come from too much tension in the throat and jaw. Tension tightens muscles and blocks the relaxed voice tones essential to a pleasing voice. A pleasing voice is of prime importance to nurses, airline hostesses, schoolteachers, doctors, lawyers and executives. It's important even to those who don't have to deal with lots of people.

A laboratory scientist recently told me that reducing the harshness in his voice made a dramatic difference in his relations with people.

Because tension shows up more in higher-pitched voices, women tend to be more susceptible to harshness. But men's voices can be just as unpleasant when tension and insensitivity take over.

Even though a person's voice may sound unpleasant to others, he may not be aware of it, because everyone is accustomed to his own voice. Unfortunately, many people react (often unconsciously) by disliking someone with a harsh voice. They never say, "You're a person I could like—but your voice gives me a pain." Restless movements and pained expressions are frequent reactions to a harsh voice.

We must admit that people normally avoid things that are unpleasant. Children and babies, who react more openly than adults, often show distress and irritation when they hear a harsh voice. A businessman who was running for Congress in the Southwest came to me for training. Strangely enough, what alerted him to his hard, raucous voice was not his awkward speaking delivery on TV but his brand-new granddaughter's reaction to his voice. "Every time I start talkin' to my sweet lil' baby she cries. My wife thinks it's my powerful voice that scares her."

People who are tense show tension in their voices. Those who have harsh, irritating voices will sound even more irritating when they become disturbed or excited.

One of my clients, a movie casting director, went about her work at a supercharged pace. She was proud of her ability to talk as tough as any film technician. And when she spoke, her voice grated on her listener's ears. She finally realized that, although successful in her career, she was failing in her home and social life.

Her first job was to learn how to relax. You can learn to relax, too. Throat tension, frequently a part of general body tension, shows up in the voice. Therefore, if you want to improve your speaking, you must start by relaxing your whole body. Twice a day, in midmorning and midafternoon, this wound-up woman secluded herself for a few minutes. She would lie on a couch or sit in a comfortable chair and stretch out, tensing every muscle in her body—to the tips of her fingers and toes. She would hold this rigid position for a slow count of ten and repeat the process two or three times. She would then lie still for several minutes, eyes shut, quietly relaxed, imagining she was riding down in an elevator.

To relax her neck and throat muscles, she slumped forward while sitting in a chair. Then she let her head drop, her jaw sag and her arms flop like a rag doll's. Next, for one to three minutes, she would very slowly and gently roll her head in a circle, alternating from left to right. Finally she would yawn for a few minutes, open her mouth wide and say such words as "clock," "squaw," "gong," "claw," and "paw." Theodore Roosevelt's famous exercise is good for increasing ease and resonance: Repeat "ding-dong, ding-dong," making the sounds ring out like a bell.

Our next job was to make her voice more gentle. Once she understood how her voice reflected her competitive attitude she was free to develop a more pleasing voice. For at least a few minutes every day she concentrated on talking slowly and gently, as though she were speaking to a baby or a puppy. As practice continued, gentleness began to pervade all she said. She felt a lot better, and people began to enjoy having her around.

Psychologists and scientists have been hard at work at various university research laboratories learning more about the human voice. Tests made at the Harvard University Psychological Laboratory show that from people's voices many personality traits can be correctly estimated about 90 per cent of the time. Studies at Kent State College, Ohio, demonstrate that a particularly unpleasant voice is likely to reveal neurotic tendencies. Better-adjusted men and women have pleasant voices, while people with neurotic tendencies often have voices with harsh and metallic sounds or with a definite nasal whine or breathiness.

A few years ago I gave a series of lectures on speaking techniques to a group of doctors. We spent a lot of time on the psychological effect of a doctor's voice. Too many doctors are so busy listening with stethoscopes to their patients' hearts that they are unaware that their patients are also listening—to the *doctors'* voices.

Dr. Paul Moses, a throat specialist at the Stanford University School of Medicine, calls attention in a *Saturday Evening Post* article to various personality clues to be found in the voice:

You can do with your voice what you do with your mind. When you want to disappear, you make your voice small. When you feel aggressive, you squeeze the opening at the top of your throat just as you flex the rest of your muscles, and your voice comes out hard and explosive. When you feel anxious, you pull in not only your horns, but also your vocal chords, and you sound strained and tense.

IS YOUR VOICE TOO LOUD?

As a harsh sound becomes louder, it also becomes more irritating. A voice habitually much louder than necessary may be a symptom of a hearing problem—in which case, of course, a doctor should be consulted. Then, any hearing difficulty taken care of, the individual is able to begin working on his voice.

The number of people who do nothing about their hearing difficulties is surprisingly large. *Time* magazine recently reported:

One out of every ten U.S. citizens is hard of hearing to some degree, doctors estimate. At least 4,000,000 have a disability severe enough to call for medical attention. But 3,000,000 of these do not seek it, prefer to go on cocking their heads, cupping their hands behind their ears, and trying to lip-read.

If you work in a noisy place all day your voice may be louder than you realize. You may be saying, "I can't even hear myself think." Because it is natural for us to hear ourselves when we talk, we speak louder than necessary in such places as factories, trains and subways. Try talking more softly—your listeners will still hear you even though you can hardly hear yourself.

Another reason for a loud voice may be unconscious imitation of a person once admired, or an attempt to compensate for feelings of inferiority. People who always shout or talk too loud may be expressing resentment: "You gotta show 'em who's boss! If you don't talk up they don't listen."

Anyone who tries to push others around with his voice is creating resistance, resentment and confusion—whether or not he realizes it. While on a suburban train recently, I couldn't help noticing a certain man in a party of six. In fact, half the people in the car couldn't help noticing him, either. He spoke in the loud voice that shouts, "See me! See me!" Annoyed by his loud talking, his fellow passengers reacted by staring and glaring at him. The shouter, however, appeared to be unaware of the situation he was creating—his need to attract attention was so great that he evidently didn't care how he got it.

I recall the first time a certain businessman came to see me. The hale and hearty, arm-around-the-shoulders type, he wished to arrange for some coaching in public speaking. Although he stood only a few feet away from me, his voice could have filled an auditorium. In the first session we tried to trace the cause of the exceptional loudness of his voice. Starting in his firm as an office boy, he had become the protégé of the president and was now the executive vice-president. The president, having guided and helped him, had earned his admiration. Once my client was alerted —and realized that the president was himself a loud and blustery man—he had the clue to his own loudness.

If you want to experience the nerve-wracking effects of an overly loud voice, try this experiment. When other people are in the room with you, increase the volume of your radio or TV set while the announcer is speaking. Keep your finger on the volume dial and your eye on the people. You will see and hear the results as you bring up the volume! Before explaining, turn the volume down so that you can be heard.

The very first step in becoming more sensitive to voice volume should be a medical check up of your hearing. Then investigate the possibility of a psychological reason that may be causing you to speak louder than necessary. Perhaps you wish to sound authoritative. However, if you want to sound really important, a low, soft voice with speech clarity will be many times more effective. Lower your voice volume and sharpen your articulation. Clarity of speech will give you more authority than any amount of forced volume.

After you have developed sensitivity to loudness, counteract any tendency toward too loud a voice by speaking with an exaggeratedly low volume. An alert friend or family member can help you. Have the other person stand about six feet from you. Begin by speaking one sentence just above a whisper. Repeat it two or three times. If you're not clearly understood, speak a little louder. If you were understood the first time, move six more feet away, and repeat the sentence. Continue to move away as far as you reasonably can and still be heard. A twenty- to forty-foot distance is fine. Now reverse the routine. Gradually reduce the volume of your voice as the person listening comes a few feet closer. Raise your voice volume slightly when you cannot be heard.

Use your radio when you practice the following exercise, designed to help you develop sensitivity to loudness. Men should tune in to a man's voice and women to a woman's. As you increase the radio volume, repeat the speaker's words and match the loudness. It's important to try to approximate the level of volume. Then reduce the radio

volume as much as you can, and try to match this new
level. Next, adjust the volume for normal listening, and
match again. Finally, while slowly turning from the faintest
to the loudest volume, imitate in turn the voice levels you
hear. Words here aren't important—it's the volume that
counts. Some people find this exercise easier if they count
numbers. Others repeat: "I can hear you. I can hear you. I
can talk as loud as you can. I can talk as soft as you can.
I can talk louder, louder, louder. And softer, softer, softer."

As you accustom yourself to a more appropriate and
pleasing volume, you will find little if any need to speak
louder than other people do. While you are developing
maximum power with minimum effort, not only will you
find your self-esteem increasing, but—equally important—
your controlled voice will earn you more respect from the
people you know.

IS YOUR VOICE TOO NASAL?

A more widespread cause of unpleasant harshness, which
often results in metallic and somewhat grating sounds, is
"talking through the nose." The unhappy result—a twangy
nasality—is common to some New Englanders, Midwest-
erners, Southwesterners, newsboys, circus barkers, pes-
simists, worriers—and to women who think it ladylike to
keep their mouths closed while talking. If the sounds that
are normally formed in the mouth, or "front door," are
blocked, most of the breath escapes through the "back
door"—the nose.

Although people in many localities may not realize
that much of their speech is too nasal, "talking through the
nose" does add harshness to their voices.

A shrill, hard or loud voice becomes more unpleasant if
it is also nasal. However, some voices that are soft and low-
pitched can sound pleasant even with a slight nasal tendency. It is not unusual to find that one unpleasant voice

habit will cause or accompany others. Happily, the reverse is also not unusual—overcoming one voice problem can be expected to effect an over-all improvement in the voice.

The only three basic nasal sounds that should be resonated in the nose are: *m, n* and *ng.*

A good test for nasality consists of pinching the nose (causing the nasal passages to be closed off) and saying: "Two trotters plus the Jersey cow were brought to us." This sentence should be spoken clearly and with *no* vibration in the nose.

Now, pinching your nose again, say a sentence that contains many sounds that require nasal resonance. This time the *m, n* and *ng* sounds should give you a sensation of vibration in your nose. Stress these nasal sounds as you say: "Jennie is singing in the mountains at noon."

Now say, "Father Manning." You should feel the vibrations in your nose only when you say "Manning," because "Father" has no nasal sounds. Any sounds other than *m, n* and *ng* coming out through your nose indicate that your voice is too nasal.

A tendency to nasality is present when the jaw is too tight, the mouth is not open enough and the voice is pitched too high.

Keeping in mind that your hearing sense is the true guide of your voice, learn to identify the nasal and the non-nasal sounds. Put your forefingers into your ears, shutting off outside sounds, and feel the difference in vibrations when you pronounce the nasal sounds. First hum "mmm" and then "nnn"; now open your mouth and say "ahhh." Do you feel the difference? Now, looking in a mirror, exaggerate the mouth movements while you form the sounds. Open your mouth wide in the form of an O (oval).

When you talk through your nose, you may feel a sharp, twangy unpleasantness. The nose, although important, is only one of the resonating areas. If you are to develop a voice that is rich and full, you should make complete use of your other resonators—the mouth, throat and chest. The more open your mouth, the richer, fuller and lower will be your tones. Try saying "olive" while opening your lips only slightly, as in whistling. Now say it again—opening your mouth wide and really rolling out the sound. Notice the greater richness? Opening your mouth wide and exaggerating the sounds during your exercise will help you make them more pleasing in daily conversation.

Here are a few more simple exercises to help you "govern" your nasal tones. First, use this little quatrain as a check against excessive nasality. Since it contains no nasal sounds, every sound should be pronounced through the mouth only:

> Hard by the shores of far Brazil,
> We rode for pleasure, years ago;
> Led forward ever by the will
> To brave each risk, to fight each foe.

Now try the nasal sounds (*m, n, ng*) in combination with non-nasal sounds. Keep nasality out of the other sounds, especially the vowels. When you say "time," the sound "tie" should be pronounced only through the mouth.

> Tie—tie—time
> Di—dip—dim
> Nie—snipe—nine
> Rin—rim—ring
> Rrrr—run—rrrrr—rim—rrrrr—ring

Sing and hum the following sounds, changing from one to another without stopping:

> mmmmmmmmmmmmmm–ooooooooooo–
> nnnnnnnnnnnnn–ooooooooooo–
> ringoooooringoooo

Repeat a few times.

Sing these three lines, pronouncing nasal and non-nasal sounds properly:

> My bonnie lies over the ocean
> My time is your time
> Oh, what a beautiful morning!

Speak the lines below, pronouncing nasal and non-nasal sounds properly:

> I like this tie.
> I like my time clock.
> Nine o'clock and all's well.
> It's the secret of many new numbers.
> Dollars to doughnuts, the number is dim.
> Dinner at nine in the dim-out.

IS YOUR VOICE SHRILL?

If your voice is shrill, it's because your pitch is too high and often goes even higher. Throat tension causes the strained voice to sound shrill—and as the voice gets louder, it sounds more unpleasant.

The tighter the vocal cords when vibrated, the higher will be the pitch of the tone produced. But body tension also tightens the throat, squeezes the voice tones and causes shrillness. When people raise their voices in trying to be heard or when they are anxious or angry, the throat constricts and produces a shrill tone.

A high-pitched voice may sound pleasant if the sounds are well produced. But most high-pitched voices are likely to be shrill and rather thin. Women's voices, because they are about one octave higher than men's, are more often shrill. People who live and work under strained conditions and those who suffer from daily frustration will tend to have shrill voices.

Shrill voices are accompanied by dryness, irritation in the throat and voice fatigue.

As you speak, place a finger on your throat where the Adam's apple is. If your voice sounds shrill, you will feel the muscles straining and your throat constricting.

Try this tension test. Keeping your hand on your throat, try to project your voice about thirty feet. Say, "Johnny, come here!" Now say the phrase again while you test for any strain in your tongue muscle, by pressing the flat of your thumb under your chin. If you are straining, you will feel tension under your chin. You will also feel your voice coming from the top of your head and from the front part of your face.

Speak the following phrases in a loud and commanding tone, still pressing the flat of your thumb under your chin. These words are purposely chosen to bring out tension if the sounds are not produced properly.

> Ready for action!
> Forward march!
> One, two, three, four!
> Company, halt!
> Steady now, fire!

Almost every afternoon I can hear a neighbor impatiently calling her French poodle, named Soufflé. "Soufflé, Soufflé, come here!" she calls in her high-pitched voice. Often I see the little dog react by scurrying in the opposite direction. But when the woman's son calls in his low, easy voice, Soufflé comes like a flash. Dogs live by sound, and high-pitched, harsh voices make them nervous. Such sounds make humans uneasy, too, but to a lesser degree. A harsh, high pitch suggests nervousness in the speaker and is distressing, while a low pitch is soothing.

Most people talk at a pitch higher than necessary or natural to them. Women, especially, raise their voices to

a shrill pitch when they talk on the telephone or to someone who is a short distance away. In other words, the louder
you speak the more your voice will tend toward a higher
pitch. The solution is to counteract the tendency.

A high pitch in a man's voice is also unpleasant, and for
an added reason—without basis, it may suggest a lack of
virility.

Probably the most famous case of voice improvement
since Demosthenes (the Greek who overcame stuttering
and became a famed orator by practice-speaking with
pebbles in his mouth) is that of Mrs. Eleanor Roosevelt.
When she first began making public appearances as our
"First Lady," the high pitch of her voice was well known.
Realizing her handicap, she took steps to correct it. More
recently, while helping her prepare for her CBS broadcasts, I found her voice well modulated, nicely paced and
relaxed.

To reduce shrillness, become familiar with the role your
chest plays in adding vibrancy to your voice. Place your
hand on your upper chest and hum a few bars. Feel the
vibrations? Practice sounds that can be resonated in the
chest, such as:

> Alone, alone, all, all alone,
> Alone on a wide, wide sea
>
> Roll on, roll on
>
> Over and over and over
>
> Bolder and bolder and bolder

One easy way to discover where your voice is coming
from is by saying, "Hello, how are you?" The first time
you say it, put your hand on your forehead and pitch your
voice up toward your head. Next, with your hand on your
chest, pitch your words to the chest. Notice the greater
depth and richness? Trying to think "chest-tones" will

help you lower your voice. You can also develop the warm lower tones of your voice by breathing more deeply as you talk. And remember to speak softly, even when under stress.

Try a full-toned song, such as *Row, Row, Row Your Boat*, in deep, low, soft-and-easy tones. Don't try to make your voice *too* low—and don't force it. That makes for strain and hoarseness. Try for gentle, warm tones.

Remember to:
- breathe deeply and easily (from the diaphragm)
- relax your throat (glide easily into sounds)
- open your mouth (as in a yawn)
- give time to vowel sounds (exaggerate them)
- think down (and big)
- concentrate on chest resonance

Practice of phrases that have open sounds will help your voice sound round and relaxed. Try these few sentences.

The bloodhound put his paw on the stone and barked.
Now, add more powder to the flour and pour water.
The stowaway in the boat broke away from the whole crew.
It has a lot of power, and the owner wants to sell it now.

As you reduce tension and relax your throat and jaw, you will overcome any tendency to harshness in the voice, and it will reflect your most attractive and personable qualities.

Part Two

HOW TO MAKE
THE MOST
OF YOUR SPEAKING

Chapter Five

MASTER THOSE TENSIONS
TO SPEAK YOUR BEST

Tension to the right of you! Tension to the left of you! Tension within you! And everyone keeps telling you "Relax! Relax!" Of course you want to relax. You've tried and tried, but somehow your muscles become more strained than ever—like someone afraid of water trying to float. Unless you know *how* to relax, it becomes a vicious circle: more tension—more rigidity—less mobility—more fear—more tension. And tension reduces your ability to live and speak your best.

An executive who was learning how to speak in public said to me, "I'm not sure I can relax without three martinis." Of course, the martinis may relax him—and dull his senses, and probably get his "tangue tungled" up. The only real solution is to learn how to overcome tension, how to reduce its numbing effect and how to manage yourself for more confident living.

You know, of course, that the relationship between the energy you possess and the energy you use has an effect on your way of life. And if you learn how to conserve that energy so that less goes "down the drain," you will gain added power. Since tension blocks and reduces the free

flow of energy, whatever you do to control your tensions
will release more of your personal power.

Your thoughts and feelings will determine the difference
between tension and relaxation. Healthy thoughts and actions release new energy, but negative thoughts weaken
your efficiency and waste energy. Reducing muscle tension
will influence the rest of your personality and help you live
and speak more effectively.

One example of emotional and physical interaction was
pointed out by Albert Edward Wiggam:

Physiologists have shown that one reason people are touchy,
easily insulted or grieved is that they go through life with jaws
set, faces strained and muscles tense. This causes them to jump
at the slightest noise, or the slightest insult to their egos. They
say their nerves are on edge, but it is mainly their muscles, from
eyelids to toes, that are jumping. When all your muscles are relaxed and at ease, your nerves and ego will also be at ease.

When people are tense and excited, they sometimes
appear to be completely disorganized—but appearances can
be deceiving. The human nervous system is so competently
organized that during an emotional crisis everything stops
but the basic survival functions. It's almost like all traffic
coming to a halt when the fire engines race by. Since speaking is not as basic as other functions of the body (breathing and eating), an "emergency" usually short-circuits or
weakens the process of speaking. We have all experienced
the result: if we do not get too choked up to talk, our voice
trembles, we mumble, or we stutter, sputter, hem and haw.

For most of us, speaking and dealing with others creates
many tiny tensions to which we adjust almost automatically. But when we are under what is more than a normal
amount of strain for us, the crisis machinery goes into
effect (emergency) unless we understand how to master
our tensions. Such emergencies block our normal breath

balance, break up our speech rhythms and upset the normal functioning of our voices.

With typical irony George Bernard Shaw once recorded his amusing reactions to a painful crisis:

In moments of crisis my nerves act in the most extraordinary way. When utter disaster seems imminent, my whole being is instantaneously braced to avoid it; I size up the situation in a flash, set my teeth, contract my muscles, take a firm grip of myself, and—without a tremor—always do the wrong thing....

How your reactions to a crisis will affect your speaking depends on your past experience. A crisis that will cause tension in one person may occur when he talks to his boss, in another when he rises to say a few words at a meeting.

But tension has its good points, too. It acts as a fuel to activity. We try to keep ourselves under control so that tension helps us and doesn't hinder. A certain amount of tension is necessary for the performance of our everyday tasks.

Kenneth E. Appel, President of the National Commission on Mental Health, although noting the harmful effects of nervous tension, also points out that it's not always harmful or undesirable. He says:

Certain amounts motivate self-improvement or social betterment. Probably there is an optimum level of tension for each of us—too little leads to stagnation and complacency; too much to paralysis, defensive symptoms and retreat from progress and originality.

During my lecture tours, in which I speak before clubs and organizations, a brief question period is arranged. When the lecture deals with "Overcoming Your Tension While Speaking," a question often asked is how to recognize tension. How many clues to tension can you recognize in yourself?

If you can answer "Yes" to most of the following questions, tension is not a major problem in your speaking.

1. Can you sit comfortably in a chair, holding one position for one minute without moving a muscle, just breathing quietly?

2. Can you do the same while someone is talking and you are listening?

3. Can you listen to an aggressive, angry or frustrated person for five minutes without interrupting?

4. Can you speak to someone who is about twelve feet away from you without feeling that you are straining?

5. Can you speak to a large group without fumbling or feeling awkward?

6. When distressed, do you blurt out the first words that come to you, or can you wait until you calm down?

7. When someone has kept you waiting or shows up late, can you keep the conversation pleasant?

8. When someone asks you a question that puts you on the defensive, can you keep your voice fairly calm and pleasant?

9. Can you ask directions of a stranger without feeling painfully self-conscious?

10. Can you talk with your boss without nervousness or stammering?

If after answering these questions you feel that you can benefit from relaxation, begin by learning how to relax your body muscles. Stretching, a natural tension-reducing technique anyone can do easily, should help remove excess strain. Stretch all over—with all your might. Stretch till it hurts.

First, lie flat on your back or stomach on a hard surface. (A couch or bed will do but is less effective.) Stretch out your arms and legs to the tips of your fingers and toes—as far as they'll go. Hold this tense position and your breath, too, for a slow count of five. Then release the muscles and let yourself sag—just let go. Breathe in a slow rhythm, inhaling and exhaling several times. Relax, stretch again. Do this several times.

After stretching and releasing your muscles a few times, lie quietly for several minutes. Breathe deeply, slowly, rhythmically, keeping time like a grandfather's clock. Keep your eyes gently closed. Feel the silence around you. Feel yourself floating in peaceful space. Some people can get this feeling by imagining themselves going down in an elevator—down—down—down. A perfect model for you to follow is to be found in the late Professor William Lyon Phelps' autobiography:

> Every household should contain a cat, not only for decorative and domestic values, but because the cat in quiescence is medicinal to irritable, tense men and women.
> When a cat decides to rest, he not only lies down; he pours his body out on the floor like water. It is reposeful merely to watch him.

While you are on the floor, stretched out, gently turn on one side. Balance your body for a moment, and let your weight pull you so that you roll over and over. Roll over several times. Avoid forcing the turn—easy does it.

Because each person's routine causes him to use certain muscles more than others, he builds up a pattern of muscle tensions in different parts of the body. By going through your daily postures, you can identify the positions of strain that you may want to change. For instance, you may lean over a desk too long, twist your legs and feet behind chair legs or sit at odd angles. Now experiment, taking new, comfortable positions with good back support. Keep this secret of relaxation in mind: by changing your positions often enough you will avoid an accumulation of tension in any one area. For example, your eyes will not get tired so quickly if you relax your eye muscles by changing your focus every once in a while.

High-powered people under pressure can benefit from a relaxing routine that acrobats and dancers use to unlimber.

Stand up. Spread your legs far apart. Then bend forward at the waist (like the jackknife position for diving) with the arms hanging down, hands open. Bend down easily as far as you can, then straighten up just a little—until your hands are on a level with your knees. Now, by repeating these movements quickly several times, as though you had a spring in the small of your back, you will get a loose bouncing motion that will relax you. Then walk a few steps in the wobbly fashion of a gorilla.

You can even relax in your office. Push your chair away from your desk, spread your feet apart while seated and bend down from your waist, letting your head slump and your arms dangle between your knees in rag-doll fashion —stay down for thirty seconds, then repeat a few times.

An art director came to me for help in public speaking. When we studied his gestures and body movements, we found them quite rusty. And no wonder. He confessed that many unimportant details upset him—even a picture hanging off-center would make him tense. He would strive and strain to keep his world looking tidy.

Here are some exercises that helped him look at things with a more easy-going attitude—from off-balance pictures to speaking in public.

You'll see why the first one is called the "shake-shake." It's the favorite of one of the most relaxed people I know —a former boxer and dancer now almost sixty, he is as agile as a twenty-year-old athlete. Keeping your wrists loose, begin by flapping both hands as though trying to dry them in the air. Then for a while loosely throw the arms out in front—first right and then left, in rhythm—as if you're boxing with relaxed arms; let your arms pull the shoulders and body from the waist up. Next, with knees loose begin to hop up and down on a make-believe pogo stick. Keep this up while you whirl your arms round and round from the shoulder sockets, fast and free, like a pitcher winding up to throw two balls. As you hop up, make sure your arms swing upward at the same time. Go easy till you get the feel of this.

Lynn Fontanne, when asked what her favorite exercise was, answered, "Riding in taxis." However, it's a well-known fact that she keeps her figure trim by never allowing it to tighten or settle. To untie the tension knots, she wriggles from head to toe; she stretches and squirms and twists, and in this way keeps her body flexible, expressive and beautiful.

Expert golfers claim that good golf requires not power but accuracy through muscular freedom and relaxation. In fact, the most successful and happy people—whether they're football or flute players, secretaries or salesmen—are usually the most relaxed.

From my varied experience in helping people to express themselves, I have found the shoulders to be "thermometers of emotion." Your shoulders will automatically respond to whatever you feel. When you are drawn to people, your shoulders will lean toward them—but when you are repelled, you'll pull your shoulders back. When you reject an idea, you'll naturally shrug your shoulders. In fact, you respond so unconsciously with your shoulders that they automatically reveal your feelings and attitudes.

Because your basic feelings register in your shoulders, you can reduce tension in your body by relaxing your shoulders. Remember to relax your shoulders whenever you feel tension. Simply lift them as high as they will go, then let them drop. Do this a few times.

Use these three basic routines of comfort to help your-self relax while talking:

1. Calm yourself by slow, rhythmic breathing. Sigh si-lently as you exhale, and feel your body go slightly limp. Arrange to sit during this exercise so that you can give yourself to the chair.

2. Try not to talk while you are excited or tense. Let the other person take the floor—you'll have less to regret and more to gain. Moving around is a quick way to relieve tension.

3. Move your arms and legs freely; make all kinds of gestures. Walk to a window and, if convenient, open it. Straighten out papers, pull up a chair, use your handker-chief.

Slow, almost limp movements will help you relax, while rapid movements will tend to maintain tension. *Relaxed action is always a healthy outlet for tension.*

HOW TO REMOVE TENSION
FROM THE VOICE

People are often surprised to find out how easy it is to free themselves from strain. Actually, all they need do is learn how to get out of their own way. By reducing over-anxiousness they remove obstacles and improve their entire speaking process.

The mishap of a truck illustrates this point. While go-ing through a tunnel without enough clearance, a truck got wedged in. The workmen sweated and groaned as they tried to free the truck, first one way and then another. Finally, they started hacking away at the truck's top. All the while a boy of ten, watching from the sidelines, kept pulling on the foreman's sleeve and saying to him, "Mister, I know what to do." But the exasperated foreman kept waving the boy away. Finally, to give the crew a laugh, he turned to the youngster and said, "Okay, smart alec, how you gonna do it?" Said the boy quietly, "Well, how about it if you let the air out of your tires?" Maybe your obstacle is no more of a problem than "letting the air out of your tires." Here is an exercise that will ease those tired feelings and body aches and also give you smoother voice tones.

While sitting, let your head sag until it rests on your chest (gently, like a balloon rolling off a table). Raise your head again and drop it. If you are conscious of making any effort in getting your head down, you are not yet relaxing. Your chin should come to rest with a slight bounce as it comes close to your chest. Close your eyes, open your mouth, and let your jaw drop. Let your arms go limp.

Now gently roll your head round and round to loosen the neck muscles, bending your waist slightly with the motion. Repeat for a few minutes, alternating from left to right. Gently reach out as far as you can. Although you may feel a few twinges, this exercise will help relax your neck and throat.

One of the most gracious people you will ever meet is Bing Crosby. His voice has made him an American institution. The key to his singing and speaking style is "E-a-s-y does it." He literally oozes ease. You can use the same key to relax your throat and open your mouth.

Yawning is the quickest and simplest way to relax and get ready to speak. Yawn! Yawn again! Make them big and easy. If you can't yawn at will, just open your mouth wide and breathe deeply—and you will start yawning.

Follow this up by opening your mouth wide and sighing a few long "Ah's." Loosen your lips; imitate a sleepy child. Now sigh "pah-pah" several times.

If your voice squeezes itself out, sounding hard, thin or nasal, or if you're not satisfied with voice quality and your clarity is inconsistent, then you should say "Open sesame" to your jaw.

When the jaw is held too rigidly, not only is the mold

of the mouth distorted but the free-flowing manipulations of the tongue, lips and teeth are blocked. The resonance and power of the voice are muted, almost like a trumpet.

Gritting and grinding your teeth are symptoms of tension in your jaw. Talking as though you have marbles in your mouth is another sign of jaw tension.

To free your jaw, open your mouth and drop the jaw easily. Take a deep breath and say each of the following sound units:

Yah-yah-yah, yo-yo-yo, fah-bah, fah-bah, fah-bah, blee-blee, bloo-bloo, blah-blah.

Now repeat each routine in a whisper and gradually raise your voice volume until it is normal.

Repeat each of the following words a few times before going to the next one: "clock, squaw, gong, claw, paw, lowly, lily." Remember to relax and to drop the jaw.

While keeping your jaw relaxed, say, "The artist drew a fat owl."

In the days when Theodore Roosevelt did a lot of strenuous speaking during political campaigns, loudspeaker systems didn't exist. Because he would strain and lose his voice at times, he hired a voice instructor to travel with him. To develop a relaxed resonance, Roosevelt was instructed to relax his jaw while repeating the following:

Ding-dong, ding-dong, ding-dong
Ming-mong, ming-mong, ming-mong
Hong-kong, hong-kong, hong-kong
Pling-plong, pling-plong, pling-plong

In a sleepy tone sing these lines:

Sixty men on a dead man's chest
Yo-ho-ho and a bottle of rum.

While keeping the tongue free, the jaw relaxed and the mouth open, repeat:

Lahl, lawl, like
Tete, toto, tahtah, thethe, thotho, thahthah—
Nene nono, nohnah, keke, lele, rere

To free the lips, purse them and press them forward.
Then repeat:

Loo, loo, loo, loo

Then pronounce:

E, o, ah, oo

Say the following sounds with big-voiced authority:

Bebe, bobo, bahbah
Fefe, fofo, fahfah
Meme, momo, mahmah
Kwekwe, kwokwo, kwahkwah
Wheewhee, whoawhoa, whahwhah

Not only will these exercises for limbering-up and relaxation help make your voice tones rich and pleasant, they will bring a richer and more pleasant way of life.

RELAXED CONFIDENCE

Recently a client remarked: "Last night I saw Perry Como on television. He is the most relaxed person I've ever seen. I'll bet he was born that way."

While I was at CBS I used to watch Perry Como "sweating it out" to accomplish his easy speaking and singing style, and I'm sure Perry wouldn't want people mistakenly to think he was born that way. He has worked hard to become an accomplished performer. And a good deal of his relaxed delivery comes from having faith. He says, "I believe you have to have a deep feeling for whatever you do —work hard at it—and then take it easy." And he adds, "With the help of the good Lord, everything will turn out all right."

But what has faith got to do with your ability to relax? Simply this: When others are conscious of your faith in yourself, in them, and in a higher Power, your speaking poise will show it. You will have set in motion the process by which faith and relaxation build increasing confidence.

Chapter Six

THE POWER BEHIND
THE VOICE

Gene Tunney, former heavyweight champion of the world, radiates vigor and health. The sound of his voice tells the knowing listener that he exercises and breathes properly.

But don't let that fool you! Good healthy breathing does not guarantee good speaking. You can be very healthy and still not have a good voice. It is surprising to note that even professional singers who sing with good breath control do not always speak with as good breath control. The reason is that breathing for good voice support is a special skill, like driving a car or typing. As with most skills, performance improves with practice.

Breathing is one of the few involuntary body actions over which we can learn how to exercise voluntary control. Under normal conditions we breathe in an even rhythm, but the rhythm changes according to our needs. Joy, excitement, exertion, nervous stress and emergencies cause us to breathe faster and more deeply.

Proper breathing for good voice support, however, is different. Breath should be taken in quickly and easily through the mouth, then let out slowly under control of the diaphragm and stomach muscles to vibrate the vocal cords and give power to the voice. The rhythm of breathing changes with our needs in talking.

For good voice support and vocal vitality some reserve air should always be left in the lungs. The last wisps of a breath are too shallow to give supporting power.

You can test your own breathing. Whistle as long as you can on one note. You'll find that soon the whistling sound will stop, even though you still have some breath left. You may be able to squeeze out just a bit more sound, but it will be very weak. In addition, you'll be uncomfortable while you force out the sound—and forcing is ineffective. If you use the very last cubic inch of breath when you speak, your voice will be weak, lifeless and generally poor.

Singers depend entirely on proper breathing. One of the greatest Metropolitan Opera tenors of all time, Giovanni Martinelli, explained in an *Etude* magazine interview:

The breath must be deep and tranquil, and it must originate from the diaphragm and not from the upper part of the chest. Figuratively speaking, the tone must *sit on the breath*.

Good breath control gives voice support to the actor, also. When an actor is doing a characterization that can best be portrayed with a type of breathing that lacks co-ordination, he must have perfect control over his breath power. In other words, it takes a disciplined and sober actor to portray a drunk.

The artistry of Victor Moore, one of our comedy greats, illustrates this point. Some years ago, while directing Mr. Moore in some radio plays, I was intrigued by his comedy-character style. Mr. Moore's creation of his "unsure-of-myself" character was based on his technique of "improper" breathing (talking with poorly coordinated breath). His voice would come out in a "weak-stomach whine," quivering, wavering with all the overtones of the "poor soul." Although this kind of voice is good for comedy, unless you're getting paid for being funny, you'd better leave it alone.

Actually, breathing rhythm—so vital to the voice—is a major clue to the personality. Just as a breathing rhythm that is off balance hints at personality problems, so well-balanced breathing shows the coordination and self-assurance of an adjusted personality.

Breathing begins with the diaphragm muscle, which is located just above the midriff. Perhaps you should first locate the diaphragm area and press on it firmly with one hand. When you clear your throat or cough you can feel its action.

Now—as loud as a cheer leader "yells" (but go easy on your throat)—say:

> Ho, ho, ho, ho
> Go, go, go, go
> Row, row, row, row

While you are speaking you should be able to feel the action of this muscle. The diaphragm acts like a bellows that causes air to be sucked into your lungs, held and then let out. The stomach muscles in front of the diaphragm control the flow of air and release it as needed. The more sensitively developed your diaphragm and stomach muscles, the better your breath control.

To find out how smooth your breath support is and how much breath power you have, count from one to fifteen in fifteen seconds on only one breath. Pause for one second after five and again after ten. Be sure you count to fifteen without taking a second breath. Repeat until you can get to fifteen smoothly on only one breath. If you can't finish on one breath, or if your voice after three tries sounds unsteady, you'll know there's room for improvement.

Improvement starts with the re-education of your dia-

phragm. Lie flat on your back and place a heavy book on
the diaphragm area. Breathe deeply, in and out. Watch
the book rise and fall. Now remove the book, put your
hand on your diaphragm and say "P-ooo-www!" about ten
times. (Make your sounds big—like those you hear when
the small fry shoot at one another.) By this time you
should be able to feel your diaphragm working.

Now stand up and try "P-ooo-www!" again. As you make
the sound, open your mouth wide, concentrate on the diaphragm muscle and press with your hand. The more you
practice awareness of your diaphragm, the sooner will your
breath control add power and quality to your voice.

Stand with your feet apart and describe a big, wide world
with your arms, repeating, "OOOLAHH!" ten times. Elon-
gate the vowel sounds, using one full breath each time.
Try to get as much abandon as Tarzan has. Correct practice
should free your voice, help reduce rigidity and put more
vitality into your speaking.

A short time ago, CBS referred a top-notch news reporter
to me for special coaching. Dan Karasik, a newspaperman
unacquainted with broadcasting techniques, was being
groomed for assignment to the foreign-news staff. Naturally,
his voice and speaking needed some polish and more power.
His techniques in voice, speech and news commentary improved so rapidly that within a few months he was assigned
to the CBS foreign-news staff.

An exercise that this commentator enjoyed and that has
helped many other people develop the "open-space" quality
of a healthy, ringing voice is the one I've labeled "Pookah-
Pookah Talk." With your throat relaxed, mouth opened
wide and one or both hands touching your diaphragm,
imitate an important tribal chieftain. Glide up and down
with your voice as though you were saying something intelligible. Get that "big open-space" feeling! Boom out

in an easy, round voice, without forcing, the sounds that follow:

Pookah pookah loomah goo
Oolah boolah boolah boolah
Goolah goolah moolah moolah moolah
Poobah poobah poobah goonah pookah goonah goonah pookah
Loonah loonah loonah moonah moonah noonah
Sookah boonah
Poolanah pooloonah goonah sookah
Foolah cookah manah
Bamoolah soopoo donah
Loola toonga paloolah toomba
Stamook toontah looglah goonak-oompah
Gooroonah sowinah pahmpaloon poonah

Many models with "little-girl" voices have acquired bigger and fuller voice tones by practicing these sounds for five minutes a day. (Two of these beauties, who used to introduce the Jackie Gleason Show, showed improvement after practicing these sounds for only a few hours.)

When a group of executives in the same company work with me, they soon become glib enough with Pookah-Pookah Talk to make a running dialogue of it. Acting as though they understand each other, they incorporate meaningful voice inflections, facial expressions and head-shaking into their kidding routine. It helps them get rid of tension during hectic hours.

One controlled breathing rhythm that can be used almost anywhere any time helps reduce the strain that blocks good speaking. This exercise is so relaxing that some people use it to help them fall asleep. Breathe deeply and feel your chest expand. Take a full breath while counting to four, and hold for another count of four. Then let it out completely by the time you count to four. Pause without breathing for a count of four. Repeat these four steps in the same order according to your needs—perhaps several times just before giving a talk or for several minutes for general relaxation.

You can profit from another breath-control exercise that can be done almost any time. Making only a tiny opening in your mouth—as if getting ready to whistle a very high note—force your breath out in a steady, even flow. Repeat and check yourself by holding a finger about an inch away from your mouth. You can get the same effect by exhaling through a pipe stem or straw.

In another little action exercise that lets you see your progress, first hold a piece of tissue paper a few inches away from your mouth. Blow on the bottom side of the paper in a steady stream that is forceful enough to "support" and sustain it in the air. Try to keep the paper "supported" at about the same angle all the time you're blowing at it. If the paper starts to fall, it shows that you don't have enough breath power and control to sustain a steady thrust of your breath.

You might want to try the "steam-engine" exercise— a favorite of overworked congressmen and diplomats. It's very effective in developing the diaphragm and stomach muscles for controlled breath power.

In a loud whisper imitate the sound of a steam engine as the train begins to move and gain speed. Use the sounds that imitate the explosion of steam as it drives the engine. "Puff away" in different sound combinations:

Puh-puh-puh-puh   (start very slowly)
Puh-puh-puh-puh   (gain gradually)
Puh-puh-puh-puh   (increase speed)
Puh-puh-puh-puh   (more speed and fade away)

Since most people are out of breath when they reach the ends of phrases, this exercise is designed to help anyone learn to conserve breath while talking. Don't overdo—this one is strenuous. And don't try it immediately after eating.

While directing shows for CBS, it was my privilege to work with the great actress Helen Hayes, who describes her first "lesson" in proper breathing in these words:

It was Mary Garden who first made me aware of the importance of breath. I was introduced as "little Miss Hayes, the actress." Miss Garden's response was to give me a vigorous thump just above the belt. "Actress? You can't act, my child. You haven't the diaphragm of a baby." For years I could play only ingénue roles because I had only a fluffy little flapper's breath. I could never have played mature parts without the power and poise I acquired from learning how to breathe.

Now let me introduce you to whispering aloud—one of the most effective ways to develop the breath control needed for voice power. Whisper numbers, but don't keep them a secret. Whisper LOUD!

We call loud whispering expulsive or "explosive." Whisper one phrase at a time. Very loud now! Whisper any paragraph. Follow by *speaking* the same paragraph aloud. As your diaphragm muscle improves in power, continue to test your whispering ability.

A large amount of breath tends to be forced out during the first part of every phrase; practice this simple exercise to help conserve breath at the start of your phrases. Say in a loud whisper to a friend across the room:

> **Charge of the light brigade**
> **Where are you going later tonight?**
> **Please tell me when it's time to go.**

When your listener can hear you clearly, ask him to move farther away, even into another room—but make sure he can still understand you.

Use the quotations at the end of this paragraph in perfecting your skill in breath control and voice power. Begin each unit (ending with a diagonal line) in your softest voice volume—just above a whisper. Gradually increase your volume within each unit until your voice is very loud when you reach the line. To get the most out of this exercise (designed to counteract the tendency to fade at the ends of phrases), increase your voice volume as much as you can. Try not to raise your voice pitch too high as you speak louder.

You may recognize Confucius' words of wisdom that follow.

It matters not what you inquire into/ but when you inquire into a thing you must never give it up/ until you have thoroughly understood it./ It matters not what you try to think out/ but when you once try to think out a thing/ you must never give it up until you have got what you want./ It matters not what you try to carry out/ but when you once try to carry out a thing/ you must never give it up until you have done it thoroughly and well./ If another man succeed by one effort/ you will use 100 efforts./ If another man succeed by 10 efforts/ you will use 1000 efforts./ Let a man really proceed in this manner/ and though dull he will surely become intelligent./ Though weak he will surely become strong./

After several repetitions, finish by reading the entire selection in your normal voice and in your best voice delivery. Try to convey the full meaning of each thought.

For another approach to breath control, speak Galsworthy's words on beauty (below)—go as far as you can on one breath. Then in successive readings, try to increase the number of words that you say on one breath. After a little practice, mark the material for breath pauses. As you continue to practice, you may find that changing your markings helps you give a better reading. Try to perfect your reading (keeping your mind on breathing) until you feel that you are expressing the full meaning of Galsworthy's words.

Beauty means this to one person and that to the other. And yet, when any one of us has seen that which to him is beautiful, he has known an emotion which is in every case the same in kind. A ship in sail, an opening flower, a town at night, a lovely poem, leaf shadows, a child's grace, the starry skies, apple trees in spring—the thousand sights or sounds or words that evoke in us the thought of beauty—these are the drops of rain that keep the human spirit from death by drought. They are a stealing and a silent refreshment that we perhaps do not think about but which goes on all the time. Beauty is the smile on the earth's face, open to all, and needs but the eyes to see, the mood to understand.

John Galsworthy, "Candelabra"

By correct practice of the excerpt that follows, you will learn to conserve your breath power and gain a richer voice quality. When you come to a stop line, release your remaining breath—let it out in a loud sigh before taking another breath. The more unused breath you have at the end of each phrase, the better. Continue until you feel ready to deliver your "graduate" reading.

Being "contented"/ ought to mean in English,/ as it does in French,/ being pleased./ Being content with an attic/ ought not to mean being unable to move from it/ and resigned to living in it;/ it ought to mean appreciating all there is in such a position./ For true contentment/ is a real, even an active virtue/ —not only affirmative/ but creative./ It is the power of getting out of any situation/ all there is in it.

G. K. Chesterton, "A Miscellany of Men"

By limiting the breath you use to speak each phrase you will be continuously forcing your diaphragm and stomach muscles to become more energetic. But rarely will you need to speak or read aloud without having many chances to take frequent breaths, with or without punctuation marks.

When happiness or sorrow/ becomes chronic,/ then it becomes dangerous./ Permanent sorrow is produced/ by the exaggerated pictures of our imagination;/ the longer we allow ourselves to dwell in that state/ the further we drift from reality./ Permanent happiness/ tends to make most people selfish,/ oblivious of reality,/ uninterested in anything outside their own happiness./

Rom Landau, "God Is My Adventure"

As you develop breath support and gain more control, you will get "that expansive feeling" which comes with fuller breathing. Your voice will "stretch out," and its new vitality will make your speaking more distinctive.

Chapter Seven

HOW TO BUILD
A HI–FI VOICE

When Yehudi Menuhin steps on stage to give a concert, he plays on a violin worth more than $50,000. The one that Jimmy Durante squashes in his TV act can be bought for $20. Between these two violins there's a world of difference in price—but the difference in craftsmanship is infinitely greater. Menuhin's Stradivarius has a full rich resonance—Durante's fiddle produces a comedy squeak.

Your voice is an instrument that is many times more sensitive and responsive than even the finest Stradivarius. The quality of your voice becomes richer, fuller and louder through resonance. The main resonators are the throat, mouth and nasal cavities; sympathetic overtones are added by the chest and body structure. The sounds produced by the original vibrations of the vocal chords are actually less interesting than the bleat of a sheep. Without amplification and the richness created by resonance, vocal chord vibrations would sound like "empty" noises—like noises that would come from a fiddle with tautly stretched strings but without the wooden body that serves as the resonating echo chamber.

When you were a child you probably "hollered" into an

empty well or barrel. What you heard was resonance, but outside your own voice. If you play a small radio while it's inside a large bowl, you will hear enriched and amplified sounds. In a much more complex and extraordinary way your throat, mouth and nasal passages enrich and amplify the sounds made by your own voice. You can improve your resonance almost immediately by opening your mouth more when talking.

When some men first come for speaking instruction, they hardly open their mouths when they speak. I remember one in particular because he spoke with a pipe in his mouth. Even so, he made himself clearly understood. His problem was a harsh and nasal voice.

I suggested a simple experiment that you can try out, too. First, keeping his mouth closed so that his upper and lower teeth almost touched—as though talking through his teeth—he said "Who are you?" three times. Then I asked him to repeat the phrase, but with his mouth opened as wide as possible, "Joe E. Brown fashion." Finally, with his mouth opened comfortably wide, he tried it again. When he heard himself on the tape recorder, he couldn't believe that in five minutes there could be such a difference in the way he sounded. And all he had to do was to open his mouth and remove the pipe.

If you want round, full, rich tones, you must open your mouth wide enough to let the sounds roll out. You may feel strange at the beginning because you're not used to it, but a little practice in private will overcome self-consciousness. Be sure to exaggerate the vowel sounds and let the lips move freely.

If you, like many people, talk with a stiff upper lip, your resonance is reduced and your voice tones are limited. You've probably heard what happens after a trumpeter puts a cone in the trumpet opening: a thinned-down, metallic gravel-tone. In a broad sense, a similar effect is heard when a person's upper lip is inactive. In this case, the full-bodied, more expressive voice qualities remain merely underdeveloped resources.

When the upper lip is drawn tight against the teeth, the jaws remain tense; the mouth opening spreads wide but narrow. All tones produced will sound dull and flat, almost like the sounds from a cracked bell. You can add immediate resonance to your voice if you will only open your mouth when you speak; make the opening so that it looks like O, looking in a mirror to make sure your upper lip "gets into the act."

The success of many people on radio, television and movies depends on the charm of their resonant voices. One man with whom I worked closely at CBS and whose voice I remember well is the late Edwin C. Hill. When he spoke, the vibrant resonance in his voice gave you a strong sense of "drama in the news."

To feel the resonance in your own voice, try humming. Put one hand on your forehead and the other on your chest. Now "direct" your voice for head resonance—think and hum a high note; next try for a low note and feel the rich overtones in the chest; then hum gently up and down the scale. Later, hum a melody like *The Old Folks at Home*.

Whenever I see Gordon MacRae, the singing star with whom I've worked, he's usually humming a tune. Humming, we both agree, is one method of keeping the voice warm and resonant.

To add resonance to your own voice, try some good, open-throated singing. It doesn't have to be a public performance—the shower will do. Sing whatever fits your mood, but remember it's the richness of tone that counts.

Never try to force or push a tone—you will only increase harshness and reduce resonance. Instead, get the tone to "stay with you" for a split second before you send it out. "Intoning," as this kind of "tone holding" is called, allows

the tone to be properly amplified. Intoning is similar to
the "mmmmm" you intone to show your appreciation of
a taste sensation you really enjoy. When you round out
your vowels and sustain the nasal sounds, you'll add rich
quality to your voice. Practice exaggerating the vowels (the
only open sounds), intoning each of the nasal sounds (*m*,
n and *ng*) in the phrases below.

Water ... wonderful snow-cold mountain spring water
... gleaming with sunlight ... sparkling with natural
purity ... refreshing just to look at ... wonderful, snow-
capped, bright, bracing ... gleaming with rich golden
color. Sparkling with lively bubbles. Refreshing just to
look at. A one-hundred-year-old triumph. Magically
holds the natural coolness and sparkling clarity. Slow-
aging and mellowing time, too. Cool as a mountain pool.
Now in the open. A promise of more time outdoors.
More sun ... more fun.

In the following excerpt from Thomas Wolfe's *Of Time
and the River* we have a perfect collection of meaningful
names and sounds. Try saying them.

> **Where can you match the mighty music
> of their names?—The Monongahela,
> the Colorado, the Rio Grande,
> the Columbia, the Tennessee, the Hudson
> (Sweet Thames!); the Kennebec,
> the Rappahannock, the Delaware,
> the Penobscot, the Wabash,
> the Chesapeake, the Swannanoa,
> the Indian River, the Niagara (Sweet Afton!);
> the Saint Lawrence, the Susquehanna,
> the Tombigbee, the Nantahala,
> the French Broad, the Chattahoochee,
> the Arizona, and the Potomac ...**

The weather affects our lives in many ways—including the resonance in our voices. Have you noticed that when the weather is bright and clear and the humidity low you have more brightness in your tones? But on a humid day the resonance is dulled down and dampened!

You'll also find that when you're tense your resonance diminishes, but when you're relaxed it increases. A cold will cause your voice to lose resonance and to sound dull. When you are at your healthy and energetic best, people can hear it in your voice.

If you want to hear the difference between dull and bright sounds, walk into a closet and speak. The clothes in the closet will absorb much of the sound (in the same way that soundproofing materials absorb sound in broadcast studios, restaurants and public places). Now say the same words in an empty closet or small hallway, and listen to the sound as it bounces around on the nonabsorbent or "live" surface.

Good voice resonance is a balanced blend of bright and muffled qualities. When you're rested and "rarin' to go," your voice will ring out with vitality and resonance. But when you're tired or "down in the dumps," your voice will be dull—voices that are too muffled don't have enough bounce. That's the time to energize your breathing and to pump some bright, bouncing resonance into your voice.

As you continue to increase your resonance, your voice will become a finer and more expressive instrument.

Chapter Eight

THE SPEAKING POSTURE
THAT SHOWS POISE

The old proverb, "A person with a bad name is already half-hanged" applies also to "a person with poor posture who is hanging his self-esteem in public view." People only half-listen to a person whose slovenly slouch advertises, "I'm not worth much. Don't waste your time on me."

Even before people open their mouths, their postures tell us what they think of themselves. Does your posture give the impression of poise? Do people who look at you feel "Here is someone whose words I can respect"?

The first step to achieving an appearance of poise in speaking is to use a mirror for checking your standing and sitting postures, making sure that you are easily erect.

To speak your best make sure that you have a good, firm base. Spread your feet apart (about three to five inches for women, double that for men). Place one foot about one-third of its length in front of the other, with toes turned slightly out. While you're talking, let your weight fall on the middle of both feet, favoring the balls of the feet. Putting your weight equally and firmly on both feet will give you maximum speaking power. For more relaxed talking, your weight should be on one foot and shifted occasionally.

To help get your voice power off the ground, take the body position that will help give you a burst of energy. Go through the motions of dueling—charging, returning and thrusting again, saying "Charge! On guard!" Then go through the punching motions of a fighter, saying, "Take this! And that!"—but don't strain yourself. Notice the added support given your voice by the physical motion of your body.

You can transfer the beneficial effects of this exercise to your normal speaking. Whenever you speak, tense your body slightly and momentarily—as if you were about to repeat the punching and dueling movements. The muscular sensations in your body will add forcefulness to your speaking. Get the feeling of talking from your toes up. A good picture to keep in mind is a bow and arrow—your body's the bow, your voice the arrow.

When you keep your weight on your heels, you are in the weakest position for speaking. You are really placing yourself in the position that is best for receiving or listening. When you talk—even softly—use your "position of energy," the one that makes you feel like the hammer—not the anvil.

Women sometimes stand and sit with their feet so close together—in the "good child" posture—that they sacrifice basic body support. Some men take too wide a base—the "stevedore's stance." Any position that makes a person's body rigid will add harshness to his voice and reduce its power.

Try to get the feeling of standing tall and easy. The simplest exercise is one used by modeling schools. Stand in your best and most comfortable posture—keep yourself relaxed without pulling your shoulders back. Balancing a book on top of your head, walk around the room a while. If the book falls off, put it back and try again. While still walking around and keeping the book on your head, gradually relax and begin talking—count numbers, repeat words. Then, if you will stand still while talking or reading aloud, the book still on your head, you will have to hold your head fairly still. Moving the head in easy rhythm for animation is good, but punctuating with jerky noddings of the head reduces voice power and weakens the effect of your words.

A trial lawyer, a young woman, came to consult me. She wanted to improve her speaking delivery in the courts. One of the first things I did was to make her aware of her posture and the way she was holding her head. Pulling her chin up caused her to appear to be continually looking down her nose, unaware that she was giving an impression of haughtiness. She learned that by lowering her head she could avoid looking haughty as well as increase her ability to project her voice. For good voice production the chin should be held neither too high nor too low—in a horizontal position.

When you are sitting, keep your back fairly straight and lean forward slightly. Leaning too far backward or forward interferes with good speaking. If you find yourself in a comfortable chair that is too cushiony, either sit forward—away from the back support, or use a pillow to support the lower back.

When preparing people for TV-radio broadcasts, I recommend a standing position as best for voice production. However, some people find a table and chair give them a more secure feeling. If they must sit on a couch or easy chair, I suggest that a wooden board be placed under the seat cushion.

As we improve our posture control, we take on a new poise, which makes people sit up and take notice.

Broadway director Joshua Logan once told me: "There's a mental and emotional equivalent for every human physical movement or posture. If there weren't, the theater wouldn't have anything to say."

Chapter Nine

TALKING TEMPO
AND THE PAUSE
THAT REFRESHES

Fast-talking radio-TV gossipist Walter Winchell explained: "The reason I talk fast is that if I talk slowly people will be able to hear what I say and find out how dull and unimportant it really is." Of course, he was only kidding.

Walter Winchell broadcasts at a fast pace and pitches his voice high to raise the level of excitement. And to hold our attention while he pauses between items, he uses sound effects—news tickers and buzzers. Most people don't realize, however, that his talking tempo sounds faster than it actually is.

High pitch and crisp articulation give a feeling of speed; low tones and easy articulation give people a sense of ease. You'll find that the basic pace or tempo at which people talk varies from one person to another. Each person tends to talk, move and live in his own personal rhythm, an important "key" to the personality.

Do you speak at a comfortable pace? Is everything you say clearly understood? Is your tempo appropriate to the mood, meaning and purpose of your words?

Some people have a slow, drawling, even plodding, kind

of pace that gives other people the fidgets. Others have a
habit of rattling along, cluttering their words, hardly taking
time out to breathe. Some nervous talkers seem never to
pause between their phrases, making inarticulate sounds
like "er . . . oh . . . and ah" while fumbling for the next
words.

Most people, we find, usually talk too fast because of
frustration, tension or excitement. It's a known fact that
professional performers—to add excitement—will increase
their speaking tempo, as Walter Winchell does. One of the
most exciting sports announcers, Clem McCarthy, was
famous for this style. He had such a fast-action pace that
his audience had to "listen fast" to keep up with his blow-
by-blow announcing. One night when he was broadcasting
a Maxie Baer fight, Maxie, sweating and out of breath, suddenly stopped in the middle of the fourth round, leaned
over the ropes and shouted to the press box: "Hey, Clem!
Slow down! I can't keep up with you!"

While preparing Bernard Baruch for his CBS broadcasts,
I noticed that one of the outstanding traits of this great
man was that he always took his time when he spoke. As
Arnold Bennett points out in his essay, "Hustle,"

I have noticed four very marked qualities in all the great workers
and doers of my acquaintance. They are never in a hurry; they
are never late; they are calm and quiet persons; and they always
have time to spare for any job that may turn up unexpectedly.
You never hear them say, in response to an appeal: "Haven't a
moment!"

Sooner or later we all find it pays to stop long enough to
consider what the rushing is all about—especially when
we talk. "There is more to life," observed Mahatma
Gandhi, "than increasing its speed."

Investigators for the telephone company tell me the
average American often talks so fast on the phone (more

than 125 words a minute) that he's not always easily understood. New York City telephone operators daily practice speaking slowly and distinctly.

You may want to try the selection that Bell Telephone Laboratories uses in testing both speech and instruments:

Alexander Pope judiciously observed in his Essay on Criticism:

"Men must be taught as if you taught them not,
And things unknown proposed as things forgot.

"Be silent always when you doubt your sense;
And speak, though sure, with seeming diffidence!"

When I was Chief of Production for Radio Free Europe and on the Program Planning Board, I requested program producers to have speakers and announcers talk at a slower pace than usual, even if it meant sacrificing some excitement. It was important for the listeners—many tuned in secretly—to "get the message." If you talk so fast that people can't "get your message," perhaps you're wasting your breath.

If you want to be clearly understood and to give importance to what you say, learn to respect the pause. Look at a full-page magazine ad to see how blank spaces are used as pauses for the eye. Now look at an ad with little white space—one that's packed with words, complex designs and pictures that look "busy." This ad won't catch or hold as much attention.

Pauses are the essence of timing in everything people do and say. The technique of timing in speaking begins with knowing when to speak a line, how quickly to speak it, when to cut a line short, when to wait for a laugh, when to speed up the tempo of your delivery. Basically, it is sensing the audience's mood and reactions, whether you're talking to one or one thousand. Jack Benny, a master of timing, says: "Timing is not so much knowing when to speak, but when to pause. Timing is pauses."

Edward R. Murrow, an expert broadcaster, is another public personality who has a highly developed feeling for timing. His pauses can make silence sound more eloquent than his voice.

Here are some phrases to help you test your timing know-how. Speak each phrase successively in a fast, slow, and medium tempo. Notice what a great effect the pace has on the meaning. Then speak each phrase again—but now add the pauses indicated by the stop lines. Notice that emphasizing each word that is underlined gives it added importance.

> That/ changes everything.
> Where/ is everybody?
> And I'll bet you/ he never comes back.
> You came in first./ Joe came in second./ And
>   I didn't even score.

If you feel that you talk too fast, a simple way to begin to counteract this tendency is to say the first few words of every sentence very slowly. Also read aloud, doing the same.

If other people's reactions show that you're talking too slow, practice reading aloud as rapidly as you can while retaining clarity and meaning. Then after rehearsing a few anecdotes at the fastest intelligible pace—and with shorter and fewer pauses—use them in conversation. To get a better feel of rhythm, slow speakers can add more color to their expression if they will keep time to music, drum with the fingers and tap the feet. All music has a rhythm beat but some—like march music—has a dominant beat that is easier to pick up.

You can pace your talk to match your words, meaning, feeling. Good timing can make even your most ordinary words sound eloquent.

Chapter Ten

DISCOVER YOUR ABILITY
TO SPEAK
WITH DISTINCTION

John D. Rockefeller, not a man to throw money away, was happy to pay the person who had that "certain" ability, and said so:

The ability to deal with people is as purchasable a commodity as sugar or coffee. And I pay more for that ability than for any other under the sun.

Even though many people try their best to succeed in dealing with others, they often "fumble the ball" because they do not speak clearly. Clarity in speech, a result of good articulation, comes when we correctly mold our voice tones to form speech sounds.

People whose speech is difficult to understand are often puzzled and nervous in their dealings with others, which eventually reduces their self-confidence and limits their achievements.

Certain people speak with an exaggerated drawl or nervously clutter their sounds. Others don't realize they've been mumbling their way through life. Even if they do, they still may not know what to do about it. One thing is certain—slurred speech is an obstacle to living the full life. And

anyone can improve his clarity of speech—a first step
to better human relations.

"A department store can't make money if its elevator
operators are intelligible," claimed Fred Allen—without
biting his tongue. "If the shoppers were able to understand
the operators, they would get off on the right floor, go
directly to the right department, make a purchase and
leave. But if the shoppers are confused, they wander around
for hours buying other things." In his popular, puckish
style Fred was making a point he believed important—so
much of our confusion is caused by sloppy speech.

To test your own clarity, try saying some challenging
phrases out loud:

Leaves, frost crisped, break from the trees and fall.
How far are our owner's awnings allowed to stick
out?
Wait 'till you see the man you'll meet from the mint.
Fruit salad is a food, but if you prepare it, does it
make you a cook?
When the wicked witches whisk switches, which
witch whisks her switch swiftest?
The whisper of witticisms in the winter makes you
wonder which wit is wittier.
What's all the shooting about, Mr. Wurtzel?
The Troy boat arrived with a load of preshrunk shirts.
The hunting lodge looked genuinely and truly rural.

Did you feel a little tongue-tied? If your answer is "yes,"
even after a few tries, then you'll want to give your speech
a quick brush-up.

Many people seem to think that good speech comes
naturally to performers. The truth is that the speaking
skills of many great actors and actresses was average or less

than average when they started. Helen Hayes, our great lady of the theater, tells of her early experiences:

Perhaps the history of my own speech development is one of those cases of compensation. You know, they say that Johnny Weissmuller learned to be a good swimmer because he had infantile paralysis as a child.

I was fresh from Washington and had a Southern accent without even knowing it. Director Iden Payne knew there was something wrong with my diction, although he couldn't define it.

He gave me a book of Shakespeare's sonnets to read but I didn't even know that final g's existed.

Eventually I repeated "Shall I compare thee to a summer's day" for hours.

Somebody told me I ought to exercise my tongue. I took a mirror, made all the horrible faces I could think of with my tongue, twisted it all over the place.

To help my diction, I have some of my speeches and scenes recorded; when I play them back I can hear the faults and polish the speech 'til I'm satisfied.

Perhaps you're blurring your words, speaking too rapidly, causing the syllables to tumble over one another.

More likely, however, your problem is lip laziness. When I travel around the United States I hear a certain amount of slurring everywhere. Perhaps you do, too. A few that I remember may be familiar to you: "whyncha"—why don't you; "marafak"—matter of fact; "onjuice"—orange juice.

Lip laziness is prevalent in the deep South, where we hear such things as: "Ah don' keh fow inny." Yet Southern speech, when correctly spoken, is musical and charming. For instance, David Brinkley, a popular NBC news commentator who has just a trace of a soft Carolina drawl, makes his observations with assurance but not insistence.

Good Southern speech is relaxed and open—two desirable characteristics. Southerners drawl and make their vowels (a, e, i, o, u) two-toned (diphthongs); vowels are the musical letters in our alphabet. They are open sounds and easy to say—just open your mouth and let them roll out. But we get power and clarity into our speech with consonants (especially d, t, b, p, k, g, f, v, z and s), sounds that take some doing. To pronounce them properly you must really use the tongue and lips and teeth—with energy.

Lip laziness is recognized as an all-American speech fault. Some months ago a New Jersey father asked me if I could do anything to help his nineteen-year-old daughter. He said that despite good physical health she was moody and unhappy. The boys she liked were getting engaged to other girls. The father, a successful businessman and speaker, suspected that her listless, mumbling speech was part of her personality problem. Pretty but spoiled, she had never bothered to learn how to put herself across.

I suggested the father give her a parakeet, which offers a fine challenge. A parakeet will learn only if clearly enunciated phrases are systematically pronounced over and over. One phrase the girl taught Budgie, her new pet, was: "Budgie is a nice boy."

I encouraged her to spend about thirty minutes each morning in front of a mirror, energetically repeating the alphabet and certain articulation exercises. Another method she used to overcome lip laziness was whistling for five minutes every day.

Her progress was noticeable within one month. After two months, friends and acquaintances began noticing a change in her. Her parents, who tell me that she has become a different, more outgoing person, report that she has made many new friends. (And Budgie is doing fine with his talking, too!)

To brighten the clarity of your speech read aloud these tongue-twisters:

Theophilus Thistle, the thistle-sifter, sifted a sieve of unsifted thistles. If Theophilus Thistle, the thistle-sifter, sifted a sieve of unsifted thistles, where is the sieve of unsifted thistles Theophilus Thistle, the thistle-sifter, sifted?

Sister Susie's sewing shirts for soldiers.

Slippery sleds slide smoothly down the sluiceway.

A snifter of snuff is enough snuff for a sniff for the snuff-sniffer.

Talking through clenched teeth—as some impersonators do when imitating Gary Cooper—is a wonderful exercise for overcoming lazy speech. With your teeth tightly closed, you'll be forced to work your tongue and lips harder. You'll also be forced to exert more breath power. In short, this exaggerated form of energetic practice will influence your everyday speech.

Now with teeth clenched, say the tongue-twisters again —slowly at first, then rapidly. Then repeat these challenging sounds once more—but as you would normally say them—with the mouth open. The "teeth-clenching" warm-up should result in a better "normal" reading. When you think your enunciation is coming along nicely, read aloud the material on pages 95–99.

For the younger set, intrigued by interesting gimmicks, I suggest: Make up a paragraph of double-talk; then telephone a friend and ask him to try to repeat after you (stop at the pause lines) something like this:

What happlet to the portisan/ on the milliflow/ this cantaflas?/ When the fravis/ is on the komeen/ the sayviskan is kamaral.

If your friend can repeat your sounds accurately, you can be sure your speech has found itself.

Another way to test your speech clarity as well as to improve it needs the help of a friend. Begin by standing in a corner, facing the wall, and read something aloud (the news or other material). Have your friend—who is standing about ten feet in back of you (to prevent lip reading) —repeat each sentence.

Doing one paragraph at a time, first read each sentence backward, one word at a time, your friend repeating after each word. Then read forward a phrase or sentence at a time, your friend again repeating. You can make this exercise more challenging by increasing the speed of the reading. If your friend doesn't correctly repeat what you say, make another try. Marking what was not correctly understood after the first or second try will provide a useful reference.

If you don't seem to open your mouth enough when you talk (check yourself in a mirror), try the remedy prescribed here. Wrap the ends of each of two pencils (some men like to use pipe stems) with wax paper, a handkerchief or paper napkin. Holding the ends of the two pencils between your upper and lower molars (one pencil on each side of your mouth), read aloud as long as you can. Rest, and try again.

To improve your articulation and increase breath energy, whisper aloud—very loud—the numbers from one to twenty-five. Repeat three times. Then whisper one number and say the next one in a loud voice (odd numbers whispered, and even ones loud). Do three run-throughs in this fashion.

Now count to ten. Begin in a whisper and gradually increase your volume until you're speaking very loudly by "ten." Then reverse the process. Start by shouting "ten"— but this time reduce the volume until "one" is heard as a whisper.

The following paragraph contains most of the speech sounds found in our language. First read it aloud at normal speed (45–50 seconds), then rapidly. Do it once again slowly, and finish in normal tempo.

An old lighthouse keeper found an old map which he studied carefully and was able to decipher. From the peculiar lines and signs he was able to make it out only after careful study. The directions were to dig four feet from the lighthouse and five feet underground for a rare chest of treasure. So with a new pick and shovel he was sure he could follow the directions, but he found it difficult to follow the instructions exactly. However, after several tries he dug through the earth and began lifting out the box of treasure. Suddenly, he fell back as the treasure disintegrated into a thousand pieces and became nothing. That night he slept a wiser man.

If you can recite the following "speech mixer-upper," part of the test given applicants for jobs as radio-TV announcers, clearly and without making mistakes and in thirty seconds, your rating is good. If you can read it in twenty seconds without tripping, your rating is excellent.

I bought a batch of baking powder and baked a batch of biscuits. I brought a big basket of biscuits back to the bakery and baked a basket of big biscuits. Then I took the big basket of biscuits and the basket of big biscuits and mixed the big biscuits with the basket of biscuits that was next to the big basket and put a bunch of biscuits from the basket into a box. Then I took the box of mixed biscuits and a biscuit mixer and biscuit basket and brought the basket of biscuits and the box of mixed biscuits and the biscuit mixer to the bakery and opened a tin of sardines.

As you practice each of the sentences below, give special attention to the sound featured. You may be interested in knowing that these are more difficult to articulate than any other sounds in our language.

Consonants

s	When the fat's in the fire, it makes a hissing sound.
z	He's lazy, but on holidays he zips around to see his friends.
f	Fred was rough on him, but he laughed it off.
v	Leaving the old stove was a victory.
k	Come on, Buck, wake up.
g	He begged her to go while she giggled.
th	Either thank both of them—or don't bother.
zh	One provision was to paint the garage beige.
l	Phil rolled up his sleeves and pulled in the line.
r	The four bars played by the brasses were recorded over again.
w	Now the waiter knows.
wh	Why whisper when you can whistle?
m	That man was marooned during the oil boom.
n	Now the lining keeps the pine needles in.
ng	Sing that swinging song!

Vowels

i	Sit up with Kitty.
e	I'll bet we met before.
a	That man ran off with the fan.

Diphthongs (blend of vowel sounds)

ai	I sighed near the fire.
ou	Mr. Brown is downtown.
oi	The boy boiled it in oil.

After you lubricate the rusty parts of your speech with know-how and practice, see that your words are: clear but never clipped; easy but never loose-lipped; intelligible but never rushed or drawled. Then the charm and distinction of your speech will persuade people to discover your true abilities.

Chapter Eleven

HOW DO YOU
PRONOUNCE IT?

"At a supper party in London," writes Leonard Lyons, "actor John Loder was seated next to an attractive French woman who lives in Italy. Loder, who knows the country well, asked in what part she lived, and she replied, 'In ze Norz.'

" 'What beautiful lakes you have,' he said.

" 'How can you see zem?' she asked. 'Zey are under ze table.' "

We do not, however, have pronunciation difficulties only with people whose mother tongue is different from ours. In John Steinbeck's *The Grapes of Wrath* Ivy says, "Everybody sez words diffrent, Arkansas folks sez 'em diffrent and Oklahomy folks sez 'em diffrent. And we seen a lady from Massachusetts, an' she said 'em diffrentest of all. Couldn' hardly make out what she was a sayin'."

Roughly 10 per cent of Americans speak with an Eastern accent (New England and New York); 19 per cent with a Southern accent (south of the Ohio River, east of central Oklahoma and central Texas); the rest with what is known as the "general American accent."

These regional differences in American pronunciation

are becoming less and less marked for several reasons: the influence of radio, TV and movies; people travel more; many move to other parts of the country.

The difficulty that many people have in pronunciation of words comes from confusion created by the many different pronunciations they hear. The authoritative and accepted ways of pronouncing some words differ. The accepted pronunciation depends on where you live, the people you associate with and how modern your dictionary is.

The person who wants to improve his pronunciation should be guided mainly by the accepted standards set by authoritative references. He should find the visual symbols for sounds used in the international phonetic alphabet a real help. Some people prefer the diacritical markings in Webster's dictionary. You will find these two sources especially valuable in showing the proper pronunciation of unusual words and of familiar ones you're not sure of.

Some people who have never seen a certain word spelled out will unconsciously imitate one or another pronunciation. They will substitute "libery" for library, "souprise" for surprise, "hunderd" for hundred, "interduce" for introduce, "modren" for modern, "hern" for hers, "recconize" for recognize, "jest" for just, "deef" for deaf.

Other words are mispronounced when letters that don't belong are added: "ideer" for idea, "hisn" for his, "colyum" for column.

Much faulty speech is the result of poor pronunciation. In some sections of the country the *ng, t, d* and *s* are almost entirely ignored. Often other sounds are substituted for the correct one, as in "dis" for "this." Borchers and Wise's *Modern Speech*, a well-indexed reference, will help you find what the correct pronunciation is in your part of the country.

In most situations social acceptance depends upon our ability to express ourselves. A person who often mispronounces words may—unfairly—be thought to have a limited background. And in many cases those who have worked hard to develop special skills have unknowingly reduced their effectiveness.

Taking a few minutes to "look up the word" has saved many from embarrassing moments. Although most of us use the pronunciation we've grown up with, remember that language is fluid. It pays to be aware of cultural changes—they always come.

Chapter Twelve

SHARPEN YOUR HEARING
FOR BETTER SPEAKING

In a heartbreaking letter Ludwig van Beethoven wrote to his brother in 1802:

I found it impossible to say to others: "Speak louder! Shout! For I am deaf!" How could I proclaim the deficiency of a sense which ought to have been more perfect in me than in other men—a sense which I once had in the highest perfection, and beyond all save a few of my profession?

How unfortunate, you may say, for this great composer to have lost his hearing. But how much more unfortunate are those who have good hearing but do not make the most of it. The person who has not sharpened his sense of hearing is like an orchestra with a poor conductor, a ship with a faulty compass.

Our hearing acts not only as a sensitive control over our voices but is also our "receiving set" as we communicate with others. The sound, color and meaning of our voices and the way we mold our tones completely depend on our sense of hearing. As our hearing becomes more selective, our voices become more expressive. This interacting process goes on all the time.

Many of us can be grateful to the "school of hard knocks," which taught us to turn a painful experience into a program of self-improvement. As the Persian proverb puts it: "Courteous men learn courtesy from the discourteous." Some people have been spurred on to develop their voices and speaking ability as a result of listening to voices that annoyed or irritated them. Others have been inspired by the sound of pleasant, expressive voices. Whatever your incentive, you will find that sharpening your hearing will improve your speaking.

As you gain skill in grading the refinements in other people's voices, you will be cultivating your own. Learn to define the contrasts in quality, style and mood. Listen to the way actors use harsh voices for unsympathetic moods and pleasant voices to represent sympathetic qualities. By watching the same movie or play twice, you will be able to concentrate on these differences.

The sounds that surround us and that we hear frequently affect our speaking. People that we listen to frequently are bound to exert an influence on our speaking, depending upon how impressionable we are and how pleasant the sound of their voices. One interesting result of being surrounded by sounds that act as an influence revealed itself recently. NBC executives having no direct contact with the broadcasting side of operations—accountants, lawyers, business managers—told me that within a year after they joined the staff, they became aware of a definite improvement in their voice and speech.

As you sharpen your hearing and your "receiving set" becomes more selective, you can't help but tune up your speaking.

Chapter Thirteen

HOW TO RATE
YOUR SPEAKING ABILITY

The first step in rating your speaking ability is to record your voice on tape so that you can hear yourself as others hear you. Today a tape recorder is an indispensable tool—not only in rating but in developing your speaking skill. Equip yourself with enough reels of tape so that you can compare your recent recordings with earlier ones.

First record a sample of your everyday conversation—about three to five minutes. Start talking about people you know, your job, vacation. If you "go blank," just relax and be patient—it will come. For more suggestions, see page 92.

Next, choose, rehearse and record some of the practice material, including the public speaking topics, that follow. Before you begin to rate your speaking ability on the chart in this chapter, record the same material more than once. When you've got a sample of conversation and reading that you think truly represents your speaking, listen several times to everything you've recorded.

While you are rating your speaking ability, keep in mind your general attitude toward yourself. For instance, are you sometimes conscious of running yourself down—underestimating? Or do you overdo the "great guy" routine—overestimating? Be fair with yourself; the more objective you are, the better your judgment and the more rapid your improvement.

Try to share some recording sessions with one or more friends. If you can arrange to talk with them and forget the recorder is on, the recorded sample of your speaking will closely resemble your everyday conversation. You could try the "Person to Person" treatment, giving everyone a chance to do most of the talking.

Whenever you and several of your friends are recording together, you can rate one another. Be tactful, be friendly, but be honest. Exchanging comments in writing, unsigned, encourages people to offer their best suggestions.

The purpose of the following Speaking Ability Rating Chart is:
- to help you gain an overview of your present speaking ability
- to help you plan your program of speaking improvement
- to serve as a record of your progress

To get a sample of your conversational style, first record your ad lib answers to these questions. (After you've "warmed up," record again.)

1. Who is your favorite sports personality or movie star? And why? (one minute)

2. Who is your favorite friend and why? Where did you meet and how? (two minutes)

3. If you were offered a year's free vacation, where would you go and why? (two minutes)

4. What would you do if you won a hundred-foot yacht on a TV program? (three minutes)

To get a sample of your public speaking style, talk on the following topics:

1. As the new Commissioner of Motor Vehicles in your state, you are to talk to the women's club on "How to Be a Safe Driver." (three to five minutes)

2. Study a speech by a well-known person, and give the main points of that speech. Speak from notes if you wish. (one to three minutes)

3. Give a talk to high school senior girls on "Commonsense Hints on Getting and Holding a Job." (three to five minutes)

Read aloud every paragraph on this page. If you are recording, be sure to give the time and date before you begin.

(Be friendly.)
If you wish to win this convertible bus, mail this envelope to the Sweetheart Suzie Smith Company.

For heating efficiency, consult our company, world's largest installers and servicers of furnaces.

(Speak rapidly.)
A brown and yellow bird built his nest over the thatched-roof hut where the frost-crisped leaves break from the willow trees and fall helter-skelter in the snow.

(Enjoy the taste.)
Crisp, crunchy, thin and nutty—you'll love the delicious homestyle flavor of our product. It's hermetically sealed in aluminum foil and stays fresh always.

(Make it exciting.)
Here they come down the stretch neck and neck. They're riding fast and they're riding hard. And out in front on his white stallion Choo-Choo is Roy Bowers, the man who's first on the draw. It's time for fun and excitement with Roy Bowers and his Rough Riders.

READING MATERIAL FOR
SELF-RATING CHART

Mercury Nudges 81
"Much Cooler" Today

A trough of thick, moist air funneling in from the Gulf of Mexico pushed afternoon temperatures into the 80s yesterday and filled parks and sidewalks with shirt-sleeved strollers.

The day's high of 81.4 degrees was recorded at 4:30 p.m., but within an hour a dark gathering sky shut out the sun as a cold front began moving in from the Great Lakes, bringing showers and brisk west winds.

Today is expected to be fair, breezy and "much cooler," with highest temperatures in the 60s.

"The New York Times"

This is the story of Horace Sears. Horace wants to become an announcer, so he rehearses all the time. He rehearses in his house astride his hobby-horse, and Horace's horse is harassed by his rehearsing. Rehearsing makes Horace hoarse and hoarseness is even more harassing to his humble hobby-horse. Now if this hoarseness harasses Horace's horse, how it must affect Horace. Actually, it haunts Horace. His hoarseness has Horace wondering about his chances as an announcer. Yes, how to hoodoo his hoarseness is Horace's harshest problem. Being haunted, he might become a ghost writer, but there are no ghosts announcing in coast-to-coast casts. Will Horace continue to rehearse and get hoarse or will he not rehearse and hash the audition? And how will Horace's horse bear up if Horace rehearses? For the answers to these harassing questions, stay tuned until one week from today at this same time, same station.

Excerpt from **CBS Announcer's Audition**

The whippoorwill's formal name is Antrostomus vociferus, rather a forbidding mouthful of syllables. Antrostomus means "cave mouth," and vociferus means "vo-
ciferous," so the name is accurately descriptive. But the
bird's big mouth is utilitarian, since the whippoorwill
seines the night air for insects, its principal food. And
the quality of its voice is a matter of the individual bird,
of the listener's state of nerves, and of distance. When
a whippoorwill sounds off near a bedroom window at
4 a.m., it is an annoying loudmouth, but when it calls
from the middle distance at dusk it can be welcome and
even soothing, quite in tune with a country evening. It
is no songster, but its call can be almost a lullaby.

The voice of the whippoorwill varies with the individual bird. Like people, some whippoorwills have melodic voices and some have raucous voices. Nobody
knows why. Some whippoorwills sound almost as
though they could sing like a wood thrush if they really
tried. And some seem to have listened too long to a con-
gregation of crows. But to a person who heard whippoorwills in his youth and now hears them again, even
the raucous ones somehow arouse nostalgic memories.

That's the remarkable thing about whippoorwills:
once heard, they are never forgotten, and something in
the reiterated call speaks of quiet, wooded valleys lying
peaceful in the summer dusk. That's really quite an
achievement for a bird that never learns to sing more
than three notes, a nighttime bird that is seldom seen,
and a bird that is even more drab than an English spar-
row. Nobody ever forgets the whippoorwill's call.

"The New York Times"

If it hadn't been for a swinging lamp, there might
never have been such a thing as a grandfather's clock.
Four hundred years ago in the Cathedral at Pisa, in
Italy, a young scientist named Galileo measured the

swinging of the lamp by the beat of his pulse. He noticed that a large swing took the same time as a small one. This discovery of a basic principal of motion led him, years later, to the invention of a pendulum clock, but more important, it led him to other investigations into nature's laws of motion, like the law of falling bodies. From the Tower of Pisa he dropped two stones of different weights. They both reached the ground at the same time, proving that weight has no influence on the speed of falling bodies.

In all his studies, Galileo sought knowledge for its own sake. But on the foundations he laid down, others built a store of useful information about energy, mass, and motion. Galileo was only one of many scientists, before and since, who have done fundamental research —discovering the secrets of nature, acquiring knowledge that might help man's progress.*

"The greyness of the whole immense surface, the wind furrows upon the faces of the waves, the great masses of foam, tossed about and waving, like matted white locks, give to the sea in a gale an appearance of hoary age, lustreless, dull, without gleams, as though it had been created before light itself." *

But the symbols of hope are not lacking even in the greyness and bleakness of the winter sea. On land we know that the apparent lifelessness of winter is an illusion. Look closely at the bare branches of a tree, on which not the palest gleam of green can be discerned. Yet, spaced along each branch are the leaf buds, all the spring's magic of swelling green concealed and safely preserved under the insulating, overlapping lay-

* Reprinted from a Du Pont Show of the Month commercial, with permission of E. I. du Pont de Nemours & Co., Inc.
* Joseph Conrad, *The Mirror of the Sea*, Kent edition. New York: Doubleday-Page, 1925, p. 71.

ers. Pick off a piece of the rough bark of the trunk; there
you will find hibernating insects. Dig down through the
snow into the earth. There are the eggs of next summer's grasshoppers; there are the dormant seeds from
which will come the grass, the herb, the oak tree.

So, too, the lifelessness, the hopelessness, the despair
of the winter sea are an illusion. Everywhere are the as-
surances that the cycle has come to the full, containing
the means of its own renewal. There is the promise of
a new spring in the very iciness of the winter sea, in
the chilling of the water, which must, before many
weeks, become so heavy that it will plunge downward,
precipitating the overturn that is the first act in the
drama of spring. There is the promise of new life in the
small plantlike things that cling to the rocks of the
underlying bottom, the almost formless polyps from
which, in Spring, a new generation of jellyfish will bud
off and rise into the surface waters. There is unconscious
purpose in the sluggish forms of the copepods hibernating on the bottom, safe from the surface storms, life
sustained in their tiny bodies by the extra store of fat
with which they went into this winter sleep.

Already, from the gray shapes of cod that have moved,
unseen by man, through the cold sea to their spawning
places, the glassy globules of eggs are rising into the
surface waters. Even in the harsh world of the winter
sea, these eggs will begin the swift divisions by which
a granule of protoplasm becomes a living fishlet.

Most of all, perhaps, there is assurance in the fine dust
of life that remains in the surface waters, the invisible
spores of the diatoms, needing only the touch of warming sun and fertilizing chemicals to repeat the magic of
spring.

How would you like to hear a little story from London? It's about a kid who is only ten years old.... He's a city kid. He grew up on London's teeming East End, where there's nothing but the smell of burning coke, and the fog rolling in from the sea.

Then he moved to the country. And there his education began.

It was another world for this boy, and the wonders he saw impressed him so much he wrote an essay about a cow.

"A cow," says this kid from London's East End, "has six sides—right and left, up and down, front and back. It has a tail on which hangs a brush. With this," says the kid, "he sends the flies away. The head," writes the London city lad, "is for the purpose of growing horns and so his mouth can be somewhere. The horns are to butt with and the mouth to moo with. Under the cow hangs milk. It is arranged for milking. The cow," says our East End Hero, "has a fine sense of smell and one can smell it far away. This," he says, "is the reason for fresh air in the country."

The ten-year-old lad writes that a cow does not eat much but what it eats it eats twice so that it gets enough. When it is hungry it moos and when it says nothing at all, relates the boy from London's East End, "it is because its insides are full up with grass."

And there is the pathetic essay on a cow written by the ten-year-old kid from the London slums, where there's nothing but the smell of burning coke and fog rolling in from the sea.

Based on a press dispatch

SPEAKING ABILITY RATING CHART
A Guide to Self-Improvement

1. AM I SPEAKING
   WITH PROPER
   VOLUME?

	Yes—	No—	Not sure—
		Some-times	Most of the time
a. Is my voice too weak for talking to one person		—	—
b. Too weak for group of 10–25		—	—
c. Too weak for group of 25–75		—	—
d. Fading at end of phrase		—	—
e. Too loud for the telephone		—	—
f. Too loud for talking to one person		—	—
g. Too loud for group of 10–25		—	—
h. Too loud for auditorium loudspeaker		—	—

Comments:

2. DO I HAVE
   ENOUGH VOICE
   POWER?

	Yes—	No—	Not sure—
		Some-times	Most of the time
a. Is my voice too weak: too little breath		—	—
b. Too shaky: unsteady breath		—	—

	Some-times	Most of the time
c. Breathy: wasted breath	—	—
d. Thin: too little resonance	—	—
e. Muffled: too little projection	—	—

Comments:

3. DO I ARTICULATE CLEARLY?

Yes— No— Not sure—

	Some-times	Most of the time
a. Jaws too tense	—	—
b. Mumbling: careless, blurring sounds	—	—
c. Slurring: omitting sounds	—	—
d. Cluttering: telescoping sounds	—	—
e. Pronunciation: adding or omitting syllables	—	—
f. Poor enunciation	—	—

Comments:

4. IS MY VOICE PLEASANT?

Yes— No— Not sure—

	Some-times	Most of the time
a. Nasal: many sounds through nose	—	—
b. Hoarse: overstrained	—	—

	Some-times	Most of the time
c. Throaty: tense throat sounds	—	—
d. Hard: forced, metallic	—	—

Comments:

5. IS MY VOICE RANGE COM-FORTABLE?

Yes— No— Not sure—

	Some-times	Most of the time
a. Too high for "home-plate" pitch	—	—
b. Too low for "home-plate" pitch	—	—

Comments:

6. DO I HAVE AN EXPRESSIVE VOICE?

Yes— No— Not sure—

	Some-times	Most of the time
a. Monotonous: little change in tone	—	—
b. Dull: colorless, lacks resonance	—	—
c. Sing-song: predictable pattern	—	—
d. Overemotional: irrita-		

	Some-times	Most of the time
tion, whining, theatrical	—	—
e. Denasalized: nasal sounds blocked	—	—
f. Husky: low, chesty tones	—	—

Comments:

7. IS MY SPEAKING
   PACE IN TUNE
   WITH MOOD AND
   MEANING?

Yes—— No—— Not sure——

	Some-times	Most of the time
a. Too hesitant	—	—
b. Too fast	—	—
c. Too slow	—	—
d. Jerky	—	—
e. Not consistent	—	—

Comments:

8. DO I MAKE THE
   MOST OF PAUSES?

Yes—— No—— Not sure——

	Some-times	Most of the time
a. Too short	—	—
b. Too long	—	—
c. Too many	—	—
d. Too few	—	—

Comments:

9. ARE MY WORDS
        WELL CHOSEN?

	Yes— No— Not sure—	
	Some- times	Most of the time
a. Too many repetitions	—	—
b. Fumbling for words: "er . . . uh"	—	—
c. Wrong meaning	—	—
d. Vague word combina- tions	—	—

Comments:

10. IS MY SPEAKING
         WELL
         ORGANIZED?

	Yes— No— Not sure—	
	Some- times	Most of the time
a. Vague thinking	—	—
b. Poor memory	—	—
c. Comments unrelated	—	—
d. Inaccurate information	—	—
e. Inadequate preparation	—	—

Comments:

11. DO I INTERPRET
         THE WRITTEN
         MATERIAL
         EFFECTIVELY?

	Yes— No— Not sure—	
	Some- times	Most of the time
a. Poor understanding of material	—	—

	Some- times	Most of the time
b. Sounds unnatural	—	—
c. Meaning not clear	—	—
d. Overdramatic: "hammy"	—	—
e. Dull, uninteresting	—	—
f. Delivery inconsistent	—	—

Comments:

12. DO I GIVE THE IM-
PRESSION OF
HAVING POISE
AND CON-
FIDENCE?

Yes— No— Not sure—

	Some- times	Most of the time
a. Awkward	—	—
b. Nervous	—	—
c. Tense	—	—
d. Labored	—	—
e. Apologetic	—	—
f. Timid	—	—
g. Dull	—	—
h. Affected	—	—
i. Sarcastic	—	—
j. Aggressive	—	—

Comments:

13. AM I ALERT,
    FRIENDLY AND
    INTERESTING IN
    CONVERSATION?   Yes— No— Not sure—
                           Some-   Most of
                           times   the time

	Sometimes	Most of the time
a. Not sure of what to say	—	—
b. Nothing much to talk about	—	—
c. Vocabulary too limited	—	—
d. Repeat pet phrases	—	—
e. Poor listener	—	—
f. Feel or act bored	—	—
g. Talk too much	—	—
h. Talk too much about self	—	—
i. Change topic abruptly	—	—
j. Give unasked-for advice	—	—
k. Monopolize conversation	—	—
l. Overbearing; overassertive statements	—	—
m. Interrupt sharply	—	—
n. Contradict awkwardly	—	—
o. Brutally frank	—	—
p. Talk things down	—	—
q. Aggressively sarcastic	—	—
r. Start arguments	—	—

Comments:

14. CAN I PREPARE AND DELIVER AN INTERESTING TALK?

	Yes___ No___ Not sure___	
	Sometimes	Most of the time
a. Not well prepared	—	—
b. Material poorly organized	—	—
c. Anecdotes poorly chosen	—	—
d. Overly tense and nervous	—	—
e. Awkward posture and gestures	—	—
f. Rhythm and timing ineffective	—	—
g. Doesn't hold attention	—	—
h. Voice and speech difficulties	—	—
i. Ineffective use of visual aids	—	—

Comments:

Part Three

WINNING VOICE QUALITIES THAT MAKE FRIENDS

Chapter Fourteen

THE VOICE PEOPLE
LIKE TO REMEMBER

The expressive voice always leaves a lasting impression. It is the essence of personal style in speaking and living. It assures, leads, warms and inspires.

While speaking before clubs and organizations, I'm sometimes asked the question: "Why do you say a pleasant voice is not enough?" My reply is similar to the one I gave the Women's City Club of Detroit not long ago: "Because a pleasant voice is only the beginning—to it must be added the life-giving qualities of color, interest, excitement."

To begin with, only after you have made your voice pleasant and flexible—an instrument in tune—will you be able to express the feelings and thoughts behind your words. The same musical score may be played by Van Cliburn and by an amateur, but it is the blending of feeling and meaning—the subtleties of modulation and tempo—that make the difference.

How responsive people think you are depends on how completely—and without inhibitions—your voice is expressing your feelings. The voices of the most admired people express friendliness, interest in others, animation, assurance and confidence—all symbols of response.

111

People don't usually pay particular attention to your voice unless it is exceptionally interesting—or irritating. Rarely will they say, "My, but she has a pleasant voice," or "That *is* an irritating voice." But they will react, as we all do, positively or negatively, according to their feelings about you.

Your voice is both a part and a symbol of your personality architecture. The importance of what you express in your voice as you deal with others, whether you realize it or not, cannot be overemphasized.

Can your voice "lift its eyebrows" when you say, "Oh, really?"

Does your voice sound sincere when you say, "I mean it."

To express yourself in a more responsive voice that will have more impact, try to become more aware of your feelings while you are talking with others. Try to put vivid meanings into your conversation. Personable speaking, like electricity, can be a powerful force. The voice power you generate and send through your "wires" of communication is up to you.

I have tried to select the voice-personality qualities most closely associated with success in dealing with others and have labeled the five that seem most desirable: authority, enthusiasm, sincerity, sympathy and romance. People who express these winning qualities are usually confident—and capable of making friends easily. What they say seems to "count" with their listeners, and it's so easy for them to influence people.

In every case good human relationships depend upon a basic sincerity essential to the expressive voice. The guarded overtones of insincerity will sooner or later be detected by others. True feelings, such as enthusiasm, sympathy and love give the voice an unmistakable freedom that reaches out to others.

Chapter Fifteen

THE VOICE
OF AUTHORITY

"Money talks," people say, but not everyone listens.

Anyway, that was the problem of a wealthy Canadian real estate man who came to see me. "When I talk," he said with a sarcastic smile, "nobody listens. Just what do I have to do to get people to listen—become a hypnotist?"

"Do you mean to tell me that *nobody* pays any attention to you?" I asked.

"Well," he chuckled, "you see, there's a lovely woman I've found, and I've been thinking of getting married again. Maybe if I could give my voice a little more 'oomph,' I can be sure she'll say 'Yes.' "

First, we went to work on his voice—to lower his pitch and give him more energetic delivery. As he began to show more authority in his voice, we began on the related "stem-to-stern" techniques: poised posture, crisp articulation and a new approach to confident conversation.

Recently I gave a talk on public speaking to the officers of the 353d Civil Affairs and Military Government Unit. An excerpt from my talk explains the techniques that develop the voice of authority.

113

"The uniform is a symbol of authority. When others in the service salute you, they salute the uniform. That is as it should be. But men who know you and work under your command will also express a certain respect in that salute for you personally. That will happen when duty and discipline are represented by an appealing person, whose orders the men enjoy following. As the name implies, a uniform makes most men look alike. You must probe deeper than the uniform if you would 'seek out and meet the man.'

"When you want to speak with true authority to anyone, it will help you to remember: True authority is slow and smooth. It never forces with the voice. Forcing, a sign of trying to compensate for a lack of self-confidence, always reduces effectiveness. You may exaggerate your lower pitch in the belief that you are giving your voice authority. In most cases, however, you are only making your tones monotonous.

"The true voice of authority—representing the desire to influence, to persuade—has assuring tones and easy, well-produced overtones. If for some reason you become frustrated in your desire to influence others and begin to push with your voice without realizing it, you're headed for negative results. By pushing with your voice, you're only revealing your unconscious attempt to force listeners to obey you. Forcing with the voice inevitably weakens your persuasive power. And even though there may be some people who can't avoid listening to you, they will secretly resist. When the other fellow's turn comes—and it will come—you will feel the force of his negative reaction."

Henry Clay Lindgren points out in his excellent book *The Art of Human Relations* that in the final analysis a boss or supervisor cannot depend entirely on his rank in dealing with subordinates. Superficially, the leader appears to be in a stronger position than the members of the group he leads. Professor Lindgren continues:

Yet, in actuality, much of his real power comes from the group. If they did not obey him, if they did not cooperate, he would fail. He would become a person with only the shadow of authority or power, because he would no longer exercise genuine control. His success lies only in being able to attract and mobilize the loyalties of his subordinates. Hence, if he does not live up to the expectations of a leader, or if he is insensitive to their needs and feelings . . . his work will be difficult or impossible, until he learns to behave as his group thinks a leader should behave, until he develops the necessary sensitivity. . . .

One of the facts of human relations which we must learn again and again as the history of the human race unfolds is that there are better and more effective ways of supervising people than through the use of direct force. Indeed, the really successful leader is one who does not have to use force at all in order to carry out his functions as a leader. . . .

Another kind of attempt at forced authority which goes "off-balance" is using a too-important tone of voice for the words. A top-heavy tone always sounds false, sometimes even foolish—and will invariably weaken whatever you say.

A speaker gains power and his listeners react positively when the tone of voice is subtle rather than overbearing.

Avoid pushing with the voice. Instead, give more time and breath support to what you say. If you can create the impression of forbearance, holding back, you will be revealing true strength.

The following excerpt, taken from *The New York Times*, comes from a short biography of a much-publicized attorney:

Mr. ——— has ample courage and aggressiveness, but since he has neither the face nor the voice of authority, his weapons are loosely limited to preparation, patience and persistence.

The man described has a boyish look and a tenor voice. His is a problem that many men have had to overcome. If you are trying to lower your pitch level, be sure not to overdo it. Begin in your middle register tones, and go lower and lower in pitch without forcing. Try a few phrases:

> Going down—going down, sir.
> We went down the canyon, down, down, down.
> You're uptown, but the meeting is to be held downtown.

To overcome monotony in your voice, vary the tones and tempo. Tone contrast is essential to everyone who wants to hold attention, to be clearly understood and to put his personality across.

Contrasting tones in speaking are as definite a "must" as the blending of negative and positive in photographs. For example, if you took an ordinary photograph and began to lighten the darks (blacks and grays) and darken the lights (whites and grays), you would lose the definition and soon blot out the entire picture. By gradually reducing the contrast between lighter and darker colors, we are left with a gray blur—and no picture. Perhaps you have experienced a similar situation while adjusting the contrast on your TV. In the same way, the voice that is limited in tone and tempo variations lacks contrast, definition and authority. It follows that the more changes in pitch, variations in volume, tone quality and tempo—the more contrast, interest and authority in the voice.

One easy way to give your voice authority is to articulate your consonants. Pay particular attention to the way you form the ends of words. Give your phrases a crisp delivery, but do not clip them. Remember, too, that rounding the vowels adds resonance to your tones and warmth to the voice of authority.

The "voice of authority" is saying, "This is definite. . . . This is important."

The clues to an authoritative voice are:

- mostly in the middle-to-lower register
- medium to slow in tempo
- intense and varied volume, but sounds best in low, quiet tones
- well-supported and firm in tone
- crisp but never sharp articulation

Put authority into your voice as you practice these phrases:

This is what we must do.

I've read the report. I approve of it one hundred per cent.

If what you say is correct, we'll have to act fast!

Wire him to take the first plane to Paris! If he doesn't make it, we'll lose the whole deal.

Okay! Go right in and let 'em have it.

I've seen what can happen. There's only one way to prevent it. We must be firm! Do you hear?

Go ahead! Shout your head off. But it won't change a thing.

In the "rigged-up" challenge that follows, you will have to "play against" the words to increase your ability to speak with authority. Many words and phrases spoken every day, not in themselves authoritative, must be spoken with the tone of authority if the meaning of the words is to be put across.

You may not be up to it. I may not be up to it.

Would you care to join us?

I can't promise you anything now.

Won't you please help me? I don't know what to do.

Do you think we can take a chance?

Chapter Sixteen

THE VOICE
OF ENTHUSIASM

Think of someone who makes you feel especially good. Ten to one it's a person whose enthusiasm is catching. Enthusiasm, although expressed in a variety of ways, can never be kept out of the voice. It's the enthusiastic voice that opens the door to people's homes and hearts. It's the voice with a lively lilt that always gives you a lift.

"Every great and commanding movement in the annals of the world is the triumph of enthusiasm," wrote Ralph Waldo Emerson. And he might have added, "No important action, however small, was ever performed without enthusiasm." Without it few things would be sold, few products made, few journeys taken. Without it, some people might not even get out of bed.

All of us have enthusiasm at times, some of us more than others. But the ideal is to develop it, to feel it, listen for it, and encourage it by becoming more responsive to others.

It's true that some people have enthusiasm to burn while others can barely manage to start the fire. When we observe those who are fortunate in having a good measure of this personality-voice quality, we find that the people who are most enthusiastic are those who are most hopeful. Enthusiasm begins with hopefulness—with a positive point of view that sets the wheels in motion and releases the vitality to keep them turning.

It is not so much a feeling of physical strength as it is your mental frame of mind—that attitude of hopefulness that will help you revive the mood of enthusiasm. It's not what you start with, it's how much you develop—and the way you use it.

True enthusiasm, used in friendly fashion, is a free form of persuasion, expressed in good faith; it is never strained or forced. Some people, so brimful of their own enthusiasm they've never taken the time to try to understand others, are puzzled by negative reactions. Being unaware of others' feelings, their tendency is to overwhelm them with enthusiasm. *Artificial* enthusiasm, characterized by loud and high-pressure talk, comes off as forced excitement and irritates others.

When properly used, the "voice of enthusiasm" attracts friends and opens the door to many opportunities. Enthusiasm, closely akin to joy as it is to hopefulness, is expressed by the voice in rising inflections and accelerating tempo.

The "voice of enthusiasm" is saying: "I appreciate things. I get a kick out of life."

The voice of enthusiasm is:
- uplifting, with a resonant quality
- varied in tempo and intensity
- varied in pitch, with rising inflections
- expressive of urgency and intensity
- always warm and vibrant

Put enthusiasm into your voice as you practice these phrases:

Boy! Look at that boat. She's a beauty.

That's the most magnificent sunset I have ever seen!

Why don't you come with us? Come on. We'll have a wonderful time.

I'm very glad to meet you. This is a pleasure; I'm delighted.

I hope to see you soon again.

Hey, what a drive! Wish I could hit the ball like you do, Harry.

Promise? Will you really do it? Oh, that's great!

I must say, I'm very proud of you.

It's just what I wanted. You couldn't have picked a nicer gift!

It's marvelous, marvelous! A true miracle.

The following phrases will be more of a challenge to you. Since the words do not "spell out" enthusiasm, you must depend more upon the tone of your voice.

Frankly, although I'm not sure what you think, I'm really not for it.

It's not what I ordered. But I'll try it on anyway.

Oh, it's raining again—always raining. Some weather!

I'd like to go there sometime, but I'm not in the mood now.

I was thinking of buying it. But your price is much too high.

He's the kind of man who—if he wants four-and-twenty blackbirds baked in a pie—twenty-three will not do.

Chapter Seventeen

THE VOICE
OF SINCERITY

Although actions may speak louder than words, people can't always see us in action. A lot depends on the sincerity with which we speak—what we say and how we say it. All good human relations are based on sincerity in the voice.

"Sincerity," writes John Tillotson, "is to speak as we think, to do as we pretend and profess, to perform what we promise, and really to be what we would seem and appear to be."

The person whose behavior is sincere has a useful asset in his voice. Sincerity always comes through in the voice.

A middle-aged woman asked me to help her prepare to give a few lectures in England on her hobby of stamp collecting. Her voice had a sing-song pattern, and a special inflection that made everything she said sound like a question. When she said, "I'm going to England in two months," she sounded as though she were asking my permission. It took her a little time to realize that she had not been coordinating her voice tones with the meaning of her words.

You can see what tricks a voice pattern can play on

meaning by misplacing the emphasis in reading the phrases that follow.

What're we going to have for supper, *Mother?* (Inflect and stress "Mother.")
What's up the road *ahead?* (Inflect and stress "ahead.")

When people speak in this manner—misplacing the emphasis—they are often misunderstood and give the impression of insincerity. The woman who was going to England told me that a friend had once tried to alert her to the impression her voice created; but not until her brother eventually convinced her that her voice did not always sound the way she thought it did was she ready to do something about it. This woman re-educated her sense of hearing, sharpened her sense of pitch and learned to counteract the false or sing-song pattern by properly matching the tone of her voice with the meaning of her words.

The "voice of sincerity" is saying, "You can believe me —trust me."

The voice of sincerity is:
• firm in tone and mostly in the middle register
• conservative in pitch variations but goes higher when anxious
• medium to soft in volume
• relatively slow in tempo with use of frequent pauses

Put sincerity into your tones as you practice these phrases.

Gentlemen, I hope you will consider this matter from another viewpoint.

I see what you mean, and I believe you, but you must see my side of the picture, too.

I must apologize for my friend. I am sure he didn't mean to say what he did.

If you look at it yourself, you'll see why it turned out like this.

The following phrases will be more of a challenge to you. Since the words do not "spell out" sincerity, you must depend upon the tone of your voice.

Well, yes, I did, but—I'm not sure now; maybe he did it.

Where do you think you're going, anyway?

If you don't want to get hurt, you'd better watch out.

If you come here again, you'll regret it.

Chapter Eighteen

THE VOICE
OF SYMPATHY

To whom do you owe the most in life? Albert Edward Wiggam, in his book *Let's Explore Your Mind,* answers:

Yourself. Your one, huge debt, which is never paid in full, is the debt you owe yourself, the debt that can be paid only by developing every trait of personality God has given you. Your first obligation is to learn to believe in yourself; your second is to learn to believe in others. If you cannot believe in yourself and do not keep your promises to yourself, you will, instead of growing in personality, become a smaller and smaller being.

Only when you believe in yourself can you believe in others. Only then will your voice have the needed support to give sympathetic understanding. Our expression of sympathy should not be limited to "feeling sorry for people," but rather should be heard in our tones of warmth and friendliness whenever we are talking with others.

Sympathy is an expression of your personal magnetism, a fact appreciated by all who have a true understanding of others. Sympathetic tones are essential to many in the professions—doctors, lawyers, teachers, clergy. Executives sensitive to the fine points of cordial business relations also recognize the importance of the sympathetic voice.

A "helping word" is no help at all unless the tone is sympathetic. Only when the voice comes forth filled with feeling do the words come to life. As Bulwer-Lytton explains,

It may, indeed, be said, that sympathy exists in all minds, as Faraday has discovered that magnetism exists in all metals; but a certain temperature is required to develop the hidden property, whether in the metal or the mind.

Nothing is more appreciated than the encouragement, the hopefulness, the uplifting quality of phrases that can be spoken every day. "I'm sorry you missed him. Won't you call again?" "You're doing fine—just fine." "We know you've been working hard and we appreciate it."

The "voice of sympathy" is saying: "I'm truly sorry. I understand how you feel. And I hope things will work out all right."

The voice of sympathy is:
- soft in volume
- soothing in tone
- of a medium pitch, with a tendency toward a lower pitch
- relatively slow in tempo, with prolonged pauses for emphasis

Put sympathy into your tones as you practice these phrases:

Yes, I know what you mean.

You're one of the nicest people I know. You really shouldn't feel like that.

Dad, I appreciate what you've done for me. I know how you feel, but I've got to have a chance to grow up on my own.

You're working hard, much too hard. Take it easy. Everything's going to be all right.

I'm very grateful for all you've done.
Oh, that poor dog. He's hurt his leg.
I'm very sorry you couldn't make it.

The following phrases will be more of a challenge to you. Since the words do not spell out "sympathy," you must depend more upon the tone of your voice.

You did mention it, I remember, but this isn't really the time.

I really can't agree with you; we couldn't find a better place than this one.

Go over there now. And do as I say.

Now we must cancel the contract.

Well, if that's what you say it was, all right.

You owe me the money, and I intend to sue you for it.

Chapter Nineteen

THE VOICE
OF ROMANCE

A gardener, his curiosity piqued as he watched a little girl leave a note in a tree, came over to take a look as soon as she skipped away. Her note read:

To anybody. I love you.

In these five simple words the little girl was showing how wise are the words of Ben Franklin: "If you would be loved, love and be lovable."

The most rewarding expression of human love is reflected by the tone of voice. The person who speaks to others with the comforting sounds that say they are liked, respected, wanted, befriended and loved is speaking in the voice of romance. The voice qualities of romance can be heard when we speak to the ones we love or tenderly to a child or in a loving tone to a puppy.

To help put more romance into your voice, trust yourself to reveal more of your feelings, leaving no feeling of affection unexpressed. You should then be able to develop more easily the voice qualities that serve to express—and in turn stimulate—the added intensity of your feelings. The expression of these newly released feelings will soon ignite the spark of response in others.

"Music is love in search of a word," said Sidney Lanier. The music of language is found in the open-toned vowel sounds. In their music the human heart hears romance. The basic warmth in song and language can be expressed only in the overtones of the vowels.

You need only listen to a song in any language to hear that the melodic tones the singer sustains are the vowel sounds. Vowel sounds are also prominent in radio and TV commercials. When knowingly delivered, these sounds have a persuasive warmth.

The soft tones of romance are really a vocal caress that tells people you like them, want to be friends, and love them for what they are.

The "voice of romance" is saying, "I think you're wonderful."

The voice of romance is:
- soothing
- full of open sounds (vowels) and resonant nasal sounds (*m, n, ng*)
- soft in tone but clearly articulated
- low-pitched, with gentle variations
- varied in tempo
- never intense but always intoned
- smooth, rich and round

Put romance into your tones as you practice these phrases:

To me you're the most beautiful woman in the world.
Won't you come look at the moon with me?
Mary, how did you like Jeff? He's very nice, isn't he?
Fine, darling, we'll take a nice long vacation.
I'm in love; I'm in love with the music, the flowers, the moon and the man in the moon. I'm in love with the whole world—just because of you.

The following phrases will be more of a challenge to you. Since the words do not spell out "romance," you must depend more upon the tone of your voice.

This happens every time! What am I going to do with you now?

Will you really do it? Frankly, I don't think you will.

Try, if you can, to think about what I'm saying.

I'm afraid we can't do a thing more than we've already done.

Part Four

WHAT IS A NEGATIVE VOICE COSTING YOU?

Chapter Twenty

HOW TO FREE
THE POSITIVE VOICE

"Jes' one li'l ol' neg'tive," said a wise old Texan, "c'n turn all your winnin's to water." Speaking with a negative voice can be a mighty big "li'l ol' neg'tive."

Some time ago a friend of mine who had bought a money-losing radio station reported, "Looked at the books today, and we're doing fine. We're cutting down our losses." A year later he happily announced that he'd converted his money-losing station into a real profit-maker.

Before anyone can "cash in" on his personality assets, he must first reduce his losses. Then he can profit from his positive personality-voice qualities.

The melody of your voice is the mirror of your mood. Your voice and the way you speak reflect all the many interacting influences of your personality.

Professor Elwood Murray, in his excellent book *The Speech Personality*, points out that voice quality more than anything else reflects all the many influences to which a person responds.

The strains and tensions of maladjustment most directly, and often completely, involve the same muscle systems as those used in speech. If these strains and tensions continue over a relatively long period of time, the poor vocal behavior becomes habitual and more or less fixed, even though the original causes of the maladjustment are no longer operative. For this reason it cannot be said that everyone who has a poor voice is also maladjusted. The present voice may be a carry-over through habit of an earlier unsatisfactory condition.

Professor Murray's observation should be of special interest to all who are not yet revealing in their voices their newly developed personal qualities.

Many people give an impression that does not represent their better qualities only because they are not "putting their best voice forward." Their voices may still be revealing traces of disappointment, aloofness, self-pity, affectation, irritability, withdrawal. And this mighty big "li'l ol' neg'tive" keeps them from attracting friends and getting the most out of life.

One of my clients, a wealthy man who came up the hard way, once told me how he learned the secret of success in dealing with people. "When I was selling," he said, "I used to spend two hours every Saturday going over my sales records. And you know what I figured out? Every time I 'muffed a sale,' it was because I got frustrated. And every time I got frustrated, I'd say something the customer resented. Then—what'd you expect—he turned me down, and that only made me more frustrated and angry.

"One day my wife said something about the way I get angry and how it shows in my voice. So I decided if I wanted to be a good salesman, I'd have to do something about my voice. It took a little time, but I finally made it. My voice began to sound calm, and I talked slow and easy —especially when I thought my pressure was going up. Soon everybody was calling me 'easy-goin' Harry.' And that's when I really began to sell."

As we all know, frustration, anger and other emotions are heard in the voice. Negative voice tones that are heard often enough will interfere with our attempts to speak with confidence and power. Fortunately, all of us can learn how to prevent frustration, moodiness, aggressiveness and other negative tones from dominating our voices.

The first step: listen to yourself on a tape recording. Wherever you live, it shouldn't be too difficult to rent a tape recorder if you don't already have one. Then begin to listen to others as you've never listened before. Soon, with the aid of the exercises suggested, you will begin to express yourself with greater freedom and deal with people more successfully.

Chapter Twenty-one

THE SHY VOICE

"You've no idea what a poor opinion I have of myself—and how little I deserve it." So spoke W. S. Gilbert of the Gilbert and Sullivan team.

How much of his tongue was in his cheek when he said it you and I will never know. But he described precisely how a shy person feels.

People who are shy reveal a quality in their voices that sounds withdrawn, thin and weak. At a disadvantage because of sensitivity, they frequently appear and sound embarrassed when talking with people. The shy voice sounds weak—mainly because of inhibited breathing and constricted articulation. A feeling of self-consciousness may show itself in hesitant speaking.

Fear or tension will cause all of us to be apprehensive, to tense our muscles and to wish we could withdraw from unpleasant situations. And all of this is heard in the voice. Dr. Paul Moses has been interested in the effects that fear and shyness have on breathing.

He points out that both the shy person and the person who is afraid have too little—or too weak—breath support. When someone is shy or afraid, he becomes tense and has a general feeling of "shrinking." His voice seems to shrink, too, and his tone will be small.

Many people who are shy try to hide their tensions, carefully controlling their gestures and body movements. Attempts to conceal self-consciousness unfortunately only increase tension and constrict the freedom of the voice. Professor Rathbone in her practical book *Teach Yourself to Relax* reminds us:

Many tense people do not appear "nervous." On the contrary, they often appear very calm. Actually, they are restrained ... because they fear that they will reveal "nervousness" by movement. They do not realize that they are increasing their tensions by holding themselves still.

The shy voice will be given greater vitality if the shy person develops lively interests in association with others. Any activity that helps him relax and feel free to express himself is good. It is a known fact that any recognition we gain for accomplishing something adds to our poise and confidence. And added assurance helps the shy person to speak up when talking and dealing with others.

To put vitality into the shy voice, remember these hints:
- meet and greet more people
- join a club or organization—volunteer for important work
- participate in sports—dances
- at a party, approach at least one stranger and start talking
- join a "little theater" or singing group
- in time, try to talk to people who've made you feel self-conscious
- learn to relax muscle tension
- increase breath control
- energize the articulation

Chapter Twenty-two

THE FATIGUED VOICE

A woman came to consult me because she was tired and embarrassed by people always asking her to repeat everything she said. She talked in the hoarse breathiness that's close to a half-whisper—the fatigued voice that often characterizes the chronic worrier.

While her voice was being recorded I complimented her on her dress. The effect was remarkable. Her tones became more definite—if only for a few minutes. After the recording session I asked how she had spent the day. She answered, "I fed my cat . . . knitted a sock . . . and took a short walk." But her voice sounded as though she'd put in a seventy-hour week.

The fatigued voice seems to come from the "depths of despair." Only when the speaker can overcome his feelings of helplessness and hopelessness do the voice tones gain clarity.

Some people have good reason to be fatigued—they never go to bed. Others never stop worrying—and so it goes. But when the fatigued voice of self-pity says: "I'm so tired—I'm ready to drop" or "What can I do? I give up," he is defeating his unconscious purpose—to get sympathy.

He is echoing the feeling in Milton's famous line: "O dark, dark, dark, amid the blaze of noon." The self-pitying person who is constantly feeling sorry for himself soon learns that others don't like to hear his sad story.

Following the Korean conflict, when Major General William F. Dean was released by his communist captors, newsmen asked what helped him most during his three years of imprisonment. He answered, "I never felt sorry for myself, and that's what licked it. Self-pity whips more people than anything else."

The sound of the fatigued voice filled with self-pity is faded, like a water color with more water than color. Throat strain and breathiness are the cause of the weak quality in the fatigued voice. There is not enough energy to vibrate the vocal chords and produce the needed resonance for a full-bodied tone. Characterized by a lifeless monotone, the fatigued voice plods along with little intensity in a slow, dragging rhythm. Statements sound vague, and the voice fades at the end of phrases.

A weary feeling causes many people to sound fatigued when they speak. The first simple suggestion is, of course, to rest and conserve energy. When people are tired, they more easily make social errors, behave awkwardly in tense situations, and even become accident prone. The fatigue factor is so important that the Automobile Club of New York lists the first rule in safe driving as: "Do not drive if you are weary, worried or irritable." Driving safely—or speaking effectively—requires every bit of your alertness. And alertness demands continuing energy.

If it's constant worry that's putting the fatigue in your voice, why not make a list of the things that are worrying you. Then make a list of all the things that you can be grateful for. You might even like to do what one of my clients did. Try to make a recording in which you tell about the good things in your life—and play it back several times whenever you need a "pick-me-up."

This client I mentioned, a young man referred to me by a psychiatrist for help in developing conversation techniques, was able to help himself in the following manner. At a time when he was feeling on top of things, he recorded "A Message to Fred"—a pep-talk to himself. While pacing back and forth vigorously, he would deliver his message in a firm voice, like an orator trying to persuade a crowd.

Then, whenever he wasn't feeling up to par, he would play and replay one or more of his recordings of "A Message to Fred" until he felt he'd turned the trick. In time, of course, he outgrew the need for these "soliloquy sermons."

Here is a sample of his "Message to Fred" recordings:

What's the matter with you, Fred? Why don't you get wise to yourself? You're not appreciating all you've got.

You've a wonderful kind wife. And Sally's the sweetest little girl in the whole wide world. You've got a good job, a nice home and a new car.

So OK, you could have a better boss. And a bigger salary. And you've got a problem paying off the house and meeting the bills. But some people have a lot more problems than you have. And maybe they're not as young and strong as you are.

He learned that whenever he started to worry he should begin to make a list of all the things he wanted to do. He kept that list handy—it helped him to divert his worry energy into work energy. When he was tired, he would sleep. But when he was up and about, he never sat around feeling sorry for himself. He put the activities he had planned and listed into action.

Whenever you need to pull your voice up by its boot-straps, remember these hints:

- lift up your head and feel tall
- make an effort to be with people who "lift you up"
- concentrate on making the most of today, and let to-morrow take care of itself
- smile, smile, smile—and laugh, too
- be more active and try to get out into the open air frequently
- speak and breathe with more energy

Chapter Twenty-three

THE IMPERSONAL VOICE

The impersonal voice erects a "cold front" in personal relations.

On occasion, a desire to be neutral and objective is reflected in an impersonal attitude and tone of voice. But a voice that is constantly impersonal serves as a protective shield. Icy and colorless voice tones usually belong to a person who cannot unbend or be himself. He is trying, perhaps unconsciously, to keep people at a distance.

Feeling the need of an air of authority, many young men adopt the "starched-collar voice"—identified by its measured, metallic, crisp tones. And this pose of importance is "starched" into their voice personalities. The "front" they have adopted makes them appear and sound efficient, brisk and sometimes even pompous.

A person who is pompous is not always aware of the impression he creates. Alec Guinness, the great English actor, who has portrayed many "starched-collar" characters, gives a whimsical but true view of pomposity: "The thing I don't like in other people is pomposity—perhaps because I have a little of it, myself."

142

The basic sound pattern of the impersonal voice tends to be monotonous, limited in voice color and inhibited in expression. Dr. Paul Moses, who has studied thousands of voice recordings and related them to the characteristics of the speakers, writes in *The Voice of Neuroses*:

Shrinking of range expresses intended matter-of-factness, cutting off any emotional color. . . . The mathematician wants to disappear as a person behind his science, and the Army officer tries to maintain distance from the enlisted men by not giving any personal touch to his words. It is easily evident that both these factors will become the expression of overcompensation in neurosis. Some emotions carry with them the reflex action of shrinking. The voice, too, shrinks in range as well as in volume.

Men who have an impersonal voice are frequently found in top positions of responsibility. Even those who have reputations as "great social mixers" may actually be, in Dickens' words, "secret and self-contained, and solitary as an oyster." Unfortunately, their pattern of inhibiting emotional expression through both gesture and voice is not conducive to truly sympathetic human relations.

For those who wish to find out if their voices sound too cold and impersonal, it may be useful to have a recording machine turned on at home or in the office whenever you're having a conversation. The idea here is to capture a sample of natural speech. Then follow with an analysis of the voice and speech while playing the recording back several times. Becoming familiar with tone quality and the possibilities of the voice for greater expression will help give more freedom and friendliness to the voice.

If you want to put some relaxing warmth and friendliness into an impersonal voice, remember these hints:
- have some fun—express your feelings
- try to be more enthusiastic
- look at people and find out what they really want

- go out of your way to be warm and sympathetic
- learn to relax
- to add warmth to your speech, soften the consonants and give time to the vowels
- breathe fully and freely; use more vocal color; put feeling into your voice

Chapter Twenty-four

THE COMPLAINING
VOICE

The law partners of an attorney named Jim told me in confidence why they had to buy him out of the firm. They were becoming nervous wrecks because of Jim's complaining voice and words. When a client wanted to discuss a problem, instead of proceeding with the case Jim would monopolize the session by complaining about his own problems.

The dominant tones heard in Jim's voice—as in most complaining voices—is a nasal whine that reflects self-pity and is marked by a tearful, peevish quality. Other speech characteristics are inadequate resonance and poor articulation.

To help a person recognize the sound of a complaining voice and to enable him to compare it with a full-bodied, pleasant, expressive voice, I ask him to make a recording. He acts out an imitation of the complaining husband or wife, complete with whimpering voice. Try these lines yourself:

"You never do anything right. I had a bad day today. Why do we have to have dinner so late? I thought we were going out tonight. Tired? Why do you always have to be tired when I want to go out? We never go anywhere any more."

Then, following with an imitation of a sweepstakes winner, he speaks in an exhilarated and positive tone of voice. Try acting the role of a sweepstakes winner:

"Wow! Am I lucky! That's more money than I ever had in my whole life! And boy, can we use it! We'll have ourselves a real vacation for once. Gosh, am I lucky! I gotta phone Joe and Mabel—we oughta have a party. And what a party that'll be! I can't get over it. All that money! Wow!"

After you have imitated the complaining and winning voices in the above monologues, make a switch. Deliver the words of the sweepstakes winner in a complaining tone. Then speak the words of the complaining husband or wife in the most positive and friendly tones. Of course, these turnabouts in words and tone are bound to sound ludicrous, but they help point up in primary color the contrasts as well as the matching of words and tones of voice. The experiment gives people who are overweight on complaints a dramatic "sound-picture" of themselves.

If you think you might benefit from developing more positive tones of voice, you may wish to try the improvement sessions described below.

Talk about any subject—gardening, stamp collecting, other hobbies, or your work—for at least one minute (three if you can). As you do, count the number of times you use the words "I, me, my, mine." You can't help making a few references to yourself, but try to keep them at a minimum. Try again and see if you can do better; any reduction should be gratifying. If you don't have a recording machine, try the exercises with a friend.

The "talking letter" to a friend or family member is also of value in improving your voice. Make a few notes before you start. Record for about one to five minutes.

One of these suggested beginnings may help you get started:

Dear Joe, I am grateful to you because . . .

Dear Helen, I like to be with you because . . .

Dear Eddie, We were so happy to have such a fine report of your work this semester . . .

Or you might speak about impersonal matters:

Dear Jeff, We got a big kick out of visiting Washington because . . .

Dear Son, You'll enjoy the trip with me because . . .

Be sure to speak in the tone and words of appreciation. Screen out complaints, and try to fill the letter with praise.

Then listen to the playback. Every time you hear a complaining tone or word—or both—make a note. Record the same "talking letter" again, making it more positive and watching the spots that you noted.

If you run out of something to say, you might wish to recall this little quatrain "Keep A-Goin'" by Frank L. Stanton:

> 'Tain't no use to sit and whine
> 'Cause the fish ain't on your line;
> Bait your hook an' keep on tryin',
> Keep a-goin'!

If you want to add more positive power to your voice, remember these hints:

- give three compliments for every one you receive—and try to give the first one
- concentrate on the good qualities of the people you know
- try some brisk walking or other physical exercise
- reduce the tendency to nasality in the voice
- speak and breathe with energy—open the mouth more

Chapter Twenty-five

THE AFFECTED VOICE

A top TV announcer, returning to the United States after an extended stay in England, asked my help because he was failing auditions for announcing jobs. He thought I could help him find the reason for this.

After he recorded several commercials, we listened to his delivery. An impressionable person with a highly developed sense of hearing, he had picked up more than a touch of an English accent. His tones had become so pear-shaped that he no longer sounded natural; his voice had become affected. It wasn't long before he overcame the affectation and recaptured his popularity.

The person whose voice is affected may have adopted this manner of speaking in an effort to impress people. The person behind the affected voice tends to be too loud, to demand attention and to be competitive. His laughter sounds "put on" and sometimes louder than necessary. All his expressions are too effusive and overly dramatic. It's a put-on posture of certain theatrical types (in and out of show business).

When performers parade vocal mannerisms and affectations, we tend to be tolerant, granting them "dramatic license." But people seem to be less generous with the average citizen who isn't in show business.

Although not necessarily unpleasant, the affected voice tones sound insincere and unsympathetic, sometimes even aggressive. Some people whose manners and voices are affected are disappointed when they find that they mainly attract people who are insincere. Obviously, this reduces the chances of a happy relationship.

To give your voice the values of sincerity and friendly sympathy, remember these hints:
- spend more time with people who are less competitive
- go easy on demands you make on yourself and others
- think more of the meaning, and depend less on the voice tones
- reduce over-precise articulation

Chapter Twenty-six

THE PRECIOUS VOICE

Some women mask their true feelings by gushing away in a precious tone of voice. It's their unconscious imitation of what they think of as a "lovable" person.

At times the lips are pursed to pout forth a bonus of baby talk. The voice tends to be high-pitched and trills in a broad sing-song pattern.

The woman with the precious voice appears over-emotional and very anxious to please. Sometimes this vocal pose is assumed by an insecure person who may be aggressive or antagonistic. The person appears to be outgoing and loving but is really tense and intense. The artificial tones and impulsively rapid rhythm give the impression that the person is playacting.

Because the words say one thing and the voice another the result is often ludicrous. A simple statement comes out in syrupy tones; an apology becomes an embarrassing confession; a compliment sounds like flattery.

If you think your voice may sound overly precious, record a conversation with a friend. Then listen to the playback over and over again, and check to see if you have any persistent artificial-sounding pattern in your voice tones.

Listen to other people and record their voices. Study the differences and apply the methods suggested.

To reduce the artificial pattern in the precious voice, remember these hints:
- listen more carefully to others
- learn to relax—stop trying so hard
- lower the pitch—reduce meaningless pitch variations
- speak with less volume
- slow down your tempo

Chapter Twenty-seven

THE IRRITABLE VOICE

Someone once said, "You can always tell an irritable man —but you can't tell him much." A voice that is frequently irritable makes few friends.

One view of extreme irritability is described by psychiatrist Dr. Alfred Adler: "We must interpret a bad temper as the sign of an inferiority complex."

The irritable voice announces a person who is disappointed in people. His fault-finding is directed at anybody who will "take it"—wife, husband, children, salespeople, employees.

The nagging voice with its tune of tension may be set to different lyrics but can sound just as harsh. Harsh and fretful overtones come from the voice of a person who is discontented with life; and the more dissatisfied he becomes, the more reason he has to be discontented.

When Ben Franklin wrote in *Poor Richard's Almanac*: "Let thy discontents be thy secrets; if the world knows them, it will despise thee and increase them," he gave fair warning to the irritable person.

Henry Clay Lindgren in *The Art of Human Relations* states that a person is irritable because he is weighed down by anxiety and fear of failure. The more anxious he is, the more irritating he becomes—and the more he meets with resentment and resistance. The less responsive his listener, the more irritable and nagging will be his voice.

Before a person can reduce the amount of irritability in his voice, he must first try to understand himself and learn what his irritability comes from. If a person thinks an irritable tone is dominant in his voice, he may wish to try this experiment.

Write a letter to anyone who has irritated you recently. Feel free to write anything you want! Then, in the privacy of your room, read this letter aloud into a tape recorder. If you can't arrange to record it, read it aloud three times. Give it all you've got!

Once you've expressed your feelings, see if you feel less tense. As you listen to the playback, imagine that someone has sent this letter to you, and ask yourself how you would feel. Could it be that you're hurting yourself more than others?

If you are trying to keep irritation out of your voice, remember these hints:

- if possible, avoid the people who always irritate you
- concentrate on people and activities you like
- find some new friends and hobbies
- try to spend a little time every day thinking how you can help others
- relax the jaw and throat muscles, try to yawn, breathe deeply, open your mouth more
- give time to the vowels to increase the warm qualities in your voice

Chapter Twenty-eight

THE AGGRESSIVE VOICE

One of the smartest businessmen I've ever met (an office boy who became the vice-president of a large cosmetic concern) came to see me soon after he became active in politics.

He wanted to know why his public speeches were not going over. I was in the audience during his next speech, observing and analyzing his entire speaking personality. He impressed me as a rather nice person, but his voice was aggressive and overbearing—and every word was over-emphasized. He had a disagreeable way of forcing his audience to listen to him—he would stomp around, wave his arms and bang on the speaker's stand.

Later we discussed the speaking performance I had observed. During our talk he came to recognize that his aggressive voice and speaking mannerisms might earn him more enemies than votes. After a program of improvement sessions, he began to make progress in reducing the domineering tendencies in his voice. And he found a lot of satisfaction in his new and more persuasive approach to public speaking. (His wife and staff also found him much easier to get along with.)

Another client, an outstanding clubwoman, has devoted

a great deal of her time to community activities. One day it suddenly dawned on her that, despite her considerable charm, difficulties with other committee members had increased. She realized that she had become more aggressive as her work on committees grew, that her manner had become overbearing and her voice harsh and pushy. "What it all boiled down to," she said, "was that I was forgetting leaders can't be leaders unless they have followers." Soon she learned to relax and to soften her aggressive voice and manner.

To weave some soft silk into your voice, remember these hints:

- review your activities and attitudes, and reduce any tendencies to overcompensate in word or action
- try to be as easy-going as possible—make a special effort when you're frustrated
- go out of your way to be courteous and considerate of others
- learn to apply the techniques of relaxation
- give others a chance to talk while you listen patiently
- relax the throat, jaw and body muscles
- speak in a gentle voice—softly and slowly
- soften the consonants—give more time to the vowels

Part Five

THE POWERFUL
INFLUENCE OF
CONVERSATION
RELATIONS

Chapter Twenty-nine

A NEW LOOK AT
YOUR CONVERSATION
RELATIONS

Are you paying much attention to your conversation these days? Is it as modern as your clothes—as smart as your car?

People want friends and dream of success but overlook the vital key to these treasures—real "know-how" in conversation.

You can increase your influence with people and live a more colorful life—if you revitalize your conversation.

Every day, every hour, the way you talk and deal with people has more influence on your life than the cut of your clothes, the job you hold or the house you live in. With each conversation—whether it's "small talk" or a big business conference, card game or cocktails—you are making your mark and gaining a reputation. In the words of Bruce Barton, advertising executive, "For good or ill your conversation is your advertisement."

When you're having a conversation, you're not just talking—you're revealing many sides of your personality. People judge us as we judge them, by the many clues all of us give every time we have a conversation. And all of us are attracted to those people who reveal the qualities we like.

For instance, suppose you happened to meet Bing

Crosby. What quality would he be looking for? I've heard Bing, a friendly and easy-going man, say, "I like people who have a twinkle in their eyes. That means they have a sense of humor." When you meet someone, what do you look for?

In guiding people as they learn to speak with greater effectiveness, I have found over the years that the greatest obstacle to good conversation is self-centeredness. Usually the people who think and talk too much about themselves are inhibited, tense, bored—and boring.

Now ask yourself these questions. Who are the people you like best? The friends you can't wait to see again? Aren't they the ones who always make you feel good— who give you a lift? They like you for what you are. And —they make you like yourself.

The chapters that follow will help you "see yourself" in conversation, and show you how to develop the "know-how" that can make "conversation relations" a powerful influence in your life.

Chapter Thirty

CONVERSATION'S
FIRST SECRET—
LIVELY LISTENING

Screen star Marlon Brando once observed, "An actor is a guy who, if you ain't talking about him, he ain't listening." That may be true, but only some of the time. It's just that actors are people, and most people would rather talk than listen. But if people don't listen—and listening is the other half of talking—why talk?

Many problems are solved, friendships made, marriages saved, by patient and lively listening. For good conversation you need a talker and a listener. It's like baseball; every pitcher needs a catcher—and a good one. And it's even more like tennis, where the ball goes back and forth. But many people's conversations sound more like the game of golf: everyone keeps on hitting his own ball. The magic of conversation evaporates whenever people persist in talking —and resist listening.

"Americans seem to listen very little," observes English novelist Evelyn Waugh. "They talk brilliantly and wisely, with deep knowledge and apt illustrations, and I think, looking round the table, how lucky we are to be here. And looking round, I notice on every face except the speaker's a rapt, nunlike, contemplative calm. They are paying no attention at all." The disappointing result is that people talk *at* each other, or *past* each other, instead of talking *with* each other.

A sign in Senator Lyndon Johnson's Washington office reads: "You ain't learnin' when you're talkin'." The good listener recognizes that to understand accurately he must hear clearly—he must listen with "all ears."

If only people would listen as though they had to remember everything, as reporters and writers do! Could Ernest Hemingway have become a great writer without first being a great observer and listener? That's why he says, "I like to listen. I have learned a great deal from listening carefully. Most people never listen."

A young lawyer just entering the business management field came to see me about his conference and conversation relations. "More meetings, more parties, and I'm having a hard time putting myself over," was the way he said it. "When it's my turn to talk, I feel I'm not doing so well."

I asked him one of the first questions I usually ask people who consult me about conversation techniques: "Do you know how to listen?"

"What!" he exclaimed. "You're joking!"

"No-o-o," I said, "I'm not joking. Have you ever listened to anybody with all your heart and soul?" He thought a moment and replied, "Well, yeah—when I was a bomber pilot. Every time we had a briefing session my buddies and I really listened. If we didn't . . . well, you know what I mean." "There," I smiled, "that's a perfect example. Very few people have had so much depend on their ability to listen. Let's see if we can use this experience."

He gradually sharpened his listening ability and other conversation techniques. His new confidence was clearly evident in a recording I heard of one of his recent business conversations. It showed him in action and confirmed reports of his excellent progress.

Lively listening gives all of us the opportunity to see, hear and think about what's going on. It's only in those fleeting moments that we have a chance to find out what other people are like, how they feel and react. A psychologist once told me, "It's amazing how we miss so many chances for mental improvement at social gatherings by trying to keep up with several different conversations at the same time."

Recently I heard one frustrated party-goer say, "There's very little talk that's worth the listening." Perhaps you've been disappointed, too. One reason—perhaps the main one—people don't listen is because much that is said and the way it is spoken is dull. Our listening gets lazy when talkers don't have the slightest notion of how to keep people interested.

An enthusiastic person, skilled in talking, can hold your attention no matter what he says, even if he's telling about what he had for dessert or how he caught the 7:57. But the unskilled talker usually doesn't hold your attention for long—and on the rare occasions when he is successful, he can't explain why.

People who are not sensitive to the interaction of speaker and listener, whether talking or listening, will often force their conversation on others. Such an approach meets with listening resistance—the "in-one-ear-and-out-the-other" reaction.

Do you recall the Goldwynism, "Include me out?" Too many talkers—instead of including their listeners in the circle of interest—"include them out." An aggressive manner of speaking always seems to shout: "You listen to me! And that's an order!" The real speaker-and-listener harmony grows out of mutual feelings that say "you and I" and "we and us." Asking interested questions and really listening to the answers are what draws people closer together and "includes them in."

Another cause of poor listening is the lack of sympathetic feeling between speaker and listener. Lack of human warmth and interest causes people to take on that blank-eyed look. The slightest suggestion of coldness, disapproval or disrespect will cause some people to turn a "deaf ear."

One of the basic reasons for poor listening is that thought is much, much faster than speech. If the speaker does not hold our interest, our attention wanders and we lose the trend of what is being said. As we say, "our mind wanders." We get lost in our own thoughts. (Watch people's eyes; when the eyes are wandering, so are the thoughts.) Then it becomes too much of a chore to pick up where we left off. Unless we—like the bomber pilot in the briefing sessions—have a very good reason to make the effort, we become less attentive and receive less and less of the "message." We may show that we're not listening any longer by a blank look or even by a "put-on" expression of alertness—which may cover us socially but interferes with good conversation relations.

As we become more appreciative listeners, we inspire others to become more effective talkers. When we encourage others to express themselves, their own satisfaction is reflected back on us—and we become more influential speakers.

A friend of mine tells why the Duchess of Windsor is considered one of the most interesting women in the world: "It's the extraordinary way she listens. She leans forward with lively interest, breathing rapidly when the talk is exciting. Her face radiates sympathy and understanding. No one else seems to exist when her attentive eyes are on you."

Try these improvement sessions to alert your own listening habits:

BRIEF SUMMARY

With a small group, read aloud a page or less from any book. Then allow the listeners a minute or two to write a brief summary. (The fewer sentences allowed [one to three], the more challenging the assignment.) Then have each person read his summary out loud.

Repeat the same routine once or twice, reading the same page aloud again, to permit improvements in the "listener" summaries. Have the summaries of each listener read aloud again, in succession, and compare the first and third summaries of each of the several listeners. Their third tries should be quite accurate. The greater the difference between the first and third summaries of a listener, the greater his improvement in listening.

REPEAT THE MESSAGE

You can swing this with four or more in the group. One person writes out a statement, then whispers it once to the person next to him. Each person in turn whispers the message he has heard to the next person until it has gone round the circle—the last person repeating the message aloud. The message he gives is compared with the message as it was written. The more people in the circle, the greater the likelihood of the message being garbled.

For instance, suppose you'd started with: "Two canaries in a cage hopping about and singing to each other." The surprise ending might be: "Two crazy cooks on Canary Island are singing a sad song." You'll find this an amusing pastime as well as a help to your listening ability. Some families have fun with it around the dinner table.

Staying with the topic of conversation, no matter what,

has probably helped to make more salesmen presidents of their companies than any other single ability.

Five practical points subscribed to by VIPs are:

1. Reduce noise and distractions. Stay away from the phone.

2. Keep your mind on the main idea—remember to come back to it.

3. Observe and think "between the lines"—that's where the real meaning is.

4. Control your eagerness to speak—for greater gains.

5. If others must speak, let them get it out of their systems—especially if they are determined or distressed.

When you talk with people, make it count; concentrate on your listening ability. One man told me, "I made a special effort, at first, to listen carefully to every third person I talked with. Now I get more out of listening to everyone—and it's easier." Listening with a sharper ear makes you look wiser—and talk more smoothly. With it comes a poised appearance and a finer command of language. Then you'll be proud to claim, as Robert Benchley did: "Drawing on my fine command of the language, I said nothing."

Chapter Thirty-one

WHEN YOU TALK—
DO PEOPLE LISTEN?

After driving many miles across the desert in the Southwest a few years ago, I stopped at a lonesome-looking diner, ordered a cup of coffee and asked the waitress if she had any packaged crackers.

"I don' know," she drawled, "I'll see." She returned and said, "No, I reckon we don't."

"How about a glass of milk?" I asked. Her brow wrinkled. "I don' know. I'll see." She called past the counter, "Joe, we got any milk?"

After another unsuccessful try—this time for doughnuts —I settled for toast and more coffee. While waiting for my toast, a placard above the counter caught my eye. It read: "Don't ask us—if we knew the answers we wouldn't be here!"

None of us knows—or even hopes to know—*all* the answers. But those that are within our reach can increase our everyday pleasure and multiply as we reflect them in our conversation. As a psychologist once said: "Tell me how you spend your time, money, and energy, and I'll tell you how interesting you are."

A door-to-door salesman can deliver the same spiel to every housewife in town. But then he travels on—to another town. You and I, though, usually visit with the same people in the same town through the years. True, all of us find comfort in the familiar. But what is it that keeps us young and bouncy? What's one of the very best ways to get out of the musty old corner of boredom and put zing into our everyday living? Why, just build a "new-interest" wing on that "same-old-talk" house.

We put lots of effort into planning vacations—usually to "get away from it all." Vacations do help us—temporarily—to escape from the same activities, the same people, the same sameness. But the "vacations" we can take every day—the big and little things that help brighten our lives —could be anything from a walk in the woods to a new, busy activity. Before you say, "Sorry, haven't got a stitch of extra time," remember it doesn't have to be a major project. Maybe you can get a minute's worth of vacation from watching a sunrise or a sunset. Maybe just reading that book you've been putting off will do it for you. Or an hour's bowling with the boys may be your kind of "vacation." These are the big and little daily vacations that give us a lift and put new life into our conversation relations. Why not make a list of the "some day I'm going to..." plans you've been postponing. Try to get started on at least one real soon.

A woman I know develops a new interest every year. Last year she collected and learned about sea shells. This year she's brushing up on her public speaking. On next year's agenda: reading travel books and mapping out her first trip to Europe. These interests keep youth in her face and bounce in her personality—even though she's sixty-three!

Women sometimes ask, "Why is it that my husband is no longer interested in talking with me?" Perhaps part of the answer is told by Joe Hyams. In his report based on interviews with some of Europe's most glamorous personalities, he writes:

European women are far easier to talk with than Americans. This is because the European woman wants to be interesting, in contrast to the American woman, who wants to be interested. European glamor girls seem uncluttered with neuroses and are happy to discuss things other than themselves, in contradiction to Americans, who are happiest when a sympathetic ear is turned to their personal problems.

To interest others in listening to your conversation, talk less about yourself and more about them and the things they are interested in. Look for a new slant on some familiar ideas. Widen your old interests and find a few new ones. Make your word descriptions more colorful and your story-telling more lively. When you are observing something, look—then look again—as you've never looked before! What you learn this way will help you speak more accurately and put "oomph" into your conversation. Because vague words reflect vague thinking, you can clarify your thinking, and your talking, by choosing your words with greater care.

Shake out the words and phrases that everyone overworks when discussing anything and everything. "He's nice," "That's lousy," and "It's wonderful" have less and less meaning as more people use them more often. Which of these two reports interests you more: "What wonderful stories" or "These mystery stories are like the old-time thrillers—weird and wicked. Too exciting to read before bedtime?"

The late Joseph Pulitzer, publisher of *The World Telegram* for many years, remained its active publisher even after becoming blind and an invalid. When he chose his companions, Pulitzer would ask them to describe with sharp accuracy everything they saw. He would say:

Look out of the window and tell me what you see. Make me get a picture of everything—everything; never think that anything is too small to be of interest; describe every cloud, every shadow, every tree, every house, every person that passes. ...

Try to follow Joseph Pulitzer's directions for a month—it should be easier for you day by day—and notice what happens to your entire outlook on life.

A good deal of conversation is disorganized and drawn out, as though you had to enter a house by climbing in through the window and then unlocking the front door. Good talk should move along at a lively pace. Too many conversations are paced like "half-mile runs" when they should be "fifty-yard dashes."

Sloppy thinking and a cluttered arrangement of ideas will cause the talker to slip by main points but to dwell on side issues—what is called in the law courts "irrelevant material." As someone who must have been listening to a lot of vague talk observed: "How small can small talk be?"

A headwaiter confessed that he doesn't dare greet some customers with the ordinary, everyday phrase: "How are you?" These customers tell him—and in great detail. He said they made him feel that he had pulled his finger out of a dike. Once he asks, he's lost—torn between listening courteously and greeting other customers.

Most of us can take a tip from the newspapers in organizing and presenting the points we want to make in conversation. First, bring out the main points briefly (headlines), then add the necessary details. In any case, if you want to get your message across, *pinpoint* your main idea, and don't leave the subject before you do.

Do you want to increase listener interest in your conversation? Start by stopping yourself whenever you repeat any phrase you overuse. During a recent TV discussion program one panelist kept saying over and over, "As a matter of fact . . ."; another repeated, "See what I mean?"; and the moderator prefaced each remark with, "Well-er-er. . . ."

"You know," I overheard a woman on the bus saying to her companion, "some people, they're always sayin', 'See?' or 'You bet your life' or 'Boy, you ain't kiddin',' and I get tired of listenin' to it." "I'll say," chimed in her companion. "You can say that again!"

If no kind friend has told you about your own oft-re-peated phrases, you may want to check for yourself. Record a lengthy conversation on a tape or dictating machine and listen carefully for "the words you love to lean on." You should be able to spot the flat clichés and the repeated phrases that "monotonize" your conversation. Once you know what they are, the battle is half won. Make an effort —and it will be an effort at first—to avoid them as much as possible and to put no similar phrases in their places.

People frequently ask, "How can I get better acquainted with others and make friends?" One way to start is to make your first remarks inviting and personalized. Instead of saying "Hot day, isn't it?", which can be answered briefly and finally with "Yeah, sure is," try approaches like "How do you keep so cool?" or "What's your favorite swim-ming spot?" or "Do you know a good mechanic?" Of course, if you or the other person has a child or a dog along, you have a "built-in" conversation starter.

When you are in a group, it is not only polite but it also makes good sense to stick to topics that will hold the atten-tion of everyone in the group. At a recent party I heard two hi-fi enthusiasts spouting technical lingo that sounded like double talk to the other guests. ("Do you have a tweeter plus a woofer?") It was a conversation that none of the others could understand or hope to take part in. You may have been "trapped" by similar interesting but "small-focus" subjects: skin diving, chess, shell collecting. When two people in a group of six discuss a topic that calls for special knowledge, the other four will have no choice but to be silent—and probably bored—or to introduce their individual interests. Before long everyone is talking at once. And we have what can be termed a "conversational free-for-all." For instance, if women insist on recipe talk and men on hunting information, men and women end up in separate groups, which is not always desirable.

These five reminders will help you become a more interesting person and improve your conversation.

1. Jot down any anecdotes you hear and like well enough to retell. Try them out before launching them in public.

2. Increase your reading (at least two hours a week). Nonfictional topics usually give more value for time spent.

A young woman was interested in a young man whose hobby was guns. She read up on guns and could discuss his favorite topic. P.S. She became his favorite girl.

3. Look into new hobbies and activities. Even if you're short on time there are many interests that a busy person can follow in spare moments.

A friend took a high-powered telescope and a simple booklet on the stars on his vacation. The first evening he took out the telescope a whole group of vacationers lined up to have a look at the sky. While they were looking, he kept up a running commentary on the stars. After that first evening everyone greeted him as if he were the host of the resort.

4. Illustrate what you say with descriptive words.

Observe as a reporter does: hit main points first. Be specific, be brief, give details when needed.

Toss out the clichés and monotonous repetitions.

5. Consider *all* your listeners. If some aren't acquainted with what you're saying, brief them before telling about the incident: "Joe, here, and I were on the same ship during the war. And this man I'm telling about was the ship's clown—a real character. He used to. . . ."

Chapter Thirty-two

GET INTO THE SWING
OF THINGS

Have you ever attended a "jam session" where jazz musicians improvise spontaneously, without rehearsal? They hear and feel the rhythms as they "play it by ear."

Most conversations are really "verbal jam sessions." We can't anticipate what's ahead, but if we are to feel the pulse of the talk we must stay alert and wide awake.

Whether the rhythm is rapid or easy-going, lively participation—listening as well as talking—is what puts the lustre in conversation. Conversations that lack lustre don't have that swing. People who just sit and rest during conversation relax so completely that they might as well be "wall flowers." If you keep saying "I pass" all through an evening of bridge, you may as well not play. It takes energy to stay alert and in the swing—whatever the activity.

Several years ago a well-known movie star appeared as the leading man in a Broadway play written by one of my clients. When I asked how his play was doing out of town, he reported, "We had to replace the leading man. I had lunch with him just before a matinee. And he had what I was told is his usual lunch—he knocked off a few martinis and then two orders of roast duck."

173

"What?" I said in astonishment. "Just before going on-stage? What kind of performance did he give?"

"He didn't," said my friend, "he sat on stage half asleep and digested his lunch!"

. Whether the activity is acting—a highly developed skill —or good conversation, which also needs techniques to put it across, it takes energy to stay alert and "feel the pulse" of the activity. For instance, how do we know when to follow the group trend and when to "take the lead" with our own ideas? Try to "sense" the spirit of the conversation without imposing yourself. Then when the group seems to have lost interest in or resolved the previous topic, it's time to try your idea.

If it's a strain to stay in the background, every once in a while you may find yourself talking louder and more often than the others. A little astute observation should prove to anyone that people who are the most successful in persuading others are not the loud and frequent talkers— but are those who exert influence because they talk subtly and painlessly.

When you first begin to experiment with the gently per-suasive method, you may find you're not making as colorful remarks as you know you can. But be patient, have con-fidence, and with good timing you'll win out in the long run. When others are actively competing for leadership in the conversation, unless the matter is urgent let your bid ride. Challenging them head on will only throw you off balance.

Remember that people do not like to be led—if the leading is obvious. Experiments in sociology have shown that it's best for a newcomer to "take on" at first the color or tone of the group and try to harmonize with them. Then —and only then—should he attempt to lead the talk in the direction he'd like it to take.

Consider good conversation very much like a medicine

ball. Always pass it along to the next guy before it gets too heavy. If anyone holds it too long the game breaks up. Perhaps that's why many a talk-monopolizer is on the un-welcome-guest list. Once he gets to be known as "a man of a few thousand words," he remains outside the circle of good talk.

The nervous, "nonstop" talker is anxious—to be noticed. He's so thirsty for attention that he usually defeats his own purpose. Some talk-monopolizers even go so far as to an-swer their own questions. You've probably met people who remind you of the talkative woman who complained about another woman's bad manners. "I never saw anybody yawn as much as she did!" said she. "But my dear," countered her husband, "maybe she wasn't yawning. Maybe she was only trying to get a word in edgewise."

At the other extreme from the conversation monopolizer is the passive "shy clam," who says next to nothing. If he will learn to speak up, he will be agreeably surprised to find that as a conversation participant he is more highly favored than he was as a "silent sideliner."

Maybe you're one of those people who gets tongue-tied and doesn't know how to begin. You're not alone; many of us are too tense to speak up at one time or another. Just don't be too choosy with your first words. Use some phrases you've thought out beforehand as your starter. (You never go wrong when you admire someone or something.) The longer you put off speaking, the harder it is to say anything at all.

In most circumstances people find it more natural to talk than to say nothing. Say "Hello" to people, greet the mailman, be friendly with the cop on the beat.

Silence even in ordinary situations makes some people uncomfortable. But when silence can be interpreted as doubt, suspicion or even guilt, it creates difficulties between people. If you say nothing at all when you are expected to say something, some people may suspect that you dislike them. In some situations silence may even be regarded as guilt. Be sure you don't remain silent with people who may not understand—talk up, explain yourself. For instance, if you think the boss doesn't have the whole story, find the right time to tell him about it. If you think you've been misunderstood by a business associate, invite him to lunch and explain.

Don't be like the reticent old-timer who, walking down Main Street, greeted a passer-by with "Howdy," and later reported happily to his wife, "Met m' brother today—ain't seen him now in nigh onto twelve years."

If it's your turn to apologize, make it easy for yourself to say "I'm sorry." If you make a mistake, admit it. You'll feel better, and most people will understand and respect you for recognizing your error. If you're in a tight spot—talk. Even if you're nervous, saying something—almost anything—will ease the situation and help you relax.

How important are the voice and speech in conversation? Good clear speech and an expressive voice can be your trump cards! Speak loud enough—but not too loud. Listeners shouldn't have to ask you to repeat or lean forward to hear you. Avoid talking in so deliberate a manner that people will think you're picking out each word with a tweezer.

Listen to your speaking tempo. Are you speaking too slowly or too rapidly? Be alert to any annoying mannerisms that you now exhibit while talking—like hands over your mouth, saying "ummm...uh...er..." during pauses. And shouting at people puts you at a social disadvantage.

A well-known professional man, a guest at a recent gathering, suddenly flew into a rage and shouted at another guest. The atmosphere immediately became tense. He joked about it later in the evening, but his wife had a miserable time. She looked as though she could have crawled under the carpet. Such incidents are not soon forgotten. Although animation adds interest, a loud voice, violent expressions, and exaggerated facial contortions are to be avoided in all but extreme cases—such as when you have to yell "Fire!"

Using the eleven reminders that follow should help you stay in the swing of things:

1. If you want to make good in conversation, remember, before you begin, to review a few of the things you want to say and how you think you can say them best.

2. If you're going to tell a story, recall the punch line before starting.

3. Before launching a new topic, find out something interesting or unusual about it.

4. While you talk and listen, be alert to reactions. Get the feel and rhythm of the situation and stay with it.

5. Learn to ask stimulating questions with interest. It's rewarding to ask questions. People with conversation know-how do just that.

6. When asked for your opinion, keep it brief.

7. Look directly at people when you talk. Talk to everyone present. If you can't look at everyone at the same time, glance around, directing your remarks first to one and then another.

8. Make your points simply, directly and, whenever possible, in good humor.

9. Avoid looking overly serious while discussing serious matters.

10. If people are especially proud or brag of something, control any desire to "top it." When someone has just told you about his own new speedwagon, it's entirely off limits to say, "But you should see my friend's sports car!"

11. If the talk turns to religion, politics or personal matters, tread lightly—even with your best friends.

The interplay of talk and gesture, the deeper meaning of what is said, these make conversation intriguing. And the greater your sensitivity to mood and tempo, the more you will feel the pulse and purpose of conversation—and stay in the swing of things.

Chapter Thirty-three

CONVERSATION—
A KEY TO HAPPINESS
IN MARRIAGE

"Conversation without marriage? ... yes. But marriage without conversation? ... impossible!" That was the answer a family counselor gave to the question, "What happens when married people don't have much to say to each other?"

Can you measure the happiness of a marriage by the type and amount of conversation that goes on between a husband and wife?

The mutual respect and admiration of a husband and wife arise from their understanding of one another—gained largely through conversation. The late Dorothy Dix expressed the idea in these words: "The only real successful marriages are mutual admiration societies."

When couples interviewed in social-psychological surveys were asked what factors they thought were important in happy marriages, the most frequent answers were "sympathetic understanding," "a feeling of intimacy," "showing affection," "doing interesting things together." Whatever the words used, they all add up to *companionship*. How can any couple develop companionship without conversation?

179

"Before we married," reported one happily married couple, "we decided to take the 'boat boredom' test. We rented a rowboat for three consecutive Sundays and cooped ourselves up in this small space from 6 A.M. to 6 P.M. with nothing but sandwiches, soda and conversation. We decided if we could pass this test, we'd have a pretty good chance of passing the bigger test of marriage." This "boat boredom" test is a rather unusual and intriguing method of finding out what happens to mutual respect and approval when a couple is strictly on their own.

New York psychiatrist Dr. Sam Ehre says:

A permissive atmosphere is essential to every social relationship, especially marriage. Each marriage partner—by word and deed —should show a genuine interest and warm concern for the other. We all need approval and want to be accepted at face value.

Without sunshine plants perish; without sincere approval humans can lose their will to live. It is warm approval that gives life to love—and a feeling of security to husband and wife.

A marriage is happy when husband and wife have developed a pattern of words and deeds that brings them closer together. A pattern of talking over a problem when it arises, before it mounts to a crisis. Listening to each other with an earnest desire to understand, showing appreciation and interest—these are the conversation channels that should make a marriage happier.

Mutual confidence, mutual understanding, mutual admiration are the three columns that support a good marriage. E. L. Kelly, writing on "Marital Compatibility as Related to Personality Traits of Husbands and Wives" in the *Journal of Social Psychology*, found that the happier marriages are those in which the husband and wife are willing to see each other's best, most superior qualities.

The bond between marriage partners that invites each to express himself freely to the other enriches a marriage as nothing else can. In *Conceptions of Modern Psychiatry* Harry Stack Sullivan writes:

If another person matters as much to you as you do to yourself, it is quite possible to talk to this person as you have never talked to anyone before. The freedom which comes from this expanding of one's world of satisfaction to include two people, linked together by love, permits exchanges of nuances of meaning, permits investigations without fear or rebuff or humiliation. . . .

When words are guarded and few are exchanged, it's time to examine the conversation relations. The almost universal claim unhappy women make against their husbands is put into words like these: "He never listens when I talk—doesn't even answer my questions. And when I say, 'Why don't you answer my questions? Why don't you talk to me?' he just looks up and says, 'What'd you say?' "

In marriage, long silences are sometimes the severest criticism. "Speech may sometimes do harm; but so may silence, and the worse harm at that," writes Jan Struther in *A Pocket Full of Pebbles*. "No offered insult ever caused so deep a wound as a tenderness expected and withheld; and no spoken indiscretion was ever so bitterly regretted as the words that one did not speak."

Pressure of living, however, may leave too little time for talking. If your schedules don't match—and you have time only to pass one another on the way coming and going, or if your joint activities don't permit or stimulate conversation, you may not be getting the most out of marriage.

Husbands and wives who find they don't have much to talk about except household problems and office pressures may want to take a look at their activities and conversation patterns from a fresh point of view. For instance, if you're used to giving one-word ratings to the television programs you watch ("Great!" "Awful!"), try discussing the reasons for your opinions. Then as you check with your friends, your favorite TV column and other sources, you will find your conversation know-how expanding.

Husband and wife can encourage each other by listening with more interest. As Groucho Marx in one of his serious moments remarked, "One of the best hearing aids a man can have is an attentive wife." And, of course, that works both ways.

Add the spice of variety to your conversation by inviting or visiting new and stimulating friends. If your dinner parties are always in the same old groove, try costumes, games, theater parties, boat trips. When you know in advance that you're going to talk about some thing or some place, you're bound to observe more closely. Then you'll be able to describe more accurately and make your conversation more colorful. By sharing your fun and talking about it with enthusiasm, you'll get much more of a kick out of everything.

Some husbands don't find it easy to talk; they're not used to expressing themselves in words. That's the time for a wife to ask some engaging questions that will help boost hubby's self-esteem. Of course, he can do the same for the little woman. A great screen lover for many years, as well as a happily married man, the late Ronald Colman said, "A man usually falls in love with the woman who asks the kind of questions he is able to answer."

How often have we heard, almost apologetically, "I know he loves me, but he never tells me." The silent man who feels inhibited when it comes to revealing affection is denying himself and his wife the full richness of marriage.

A husband who values his wife's happiness will do his best to find the time for tender words, the little loving words that give her the deep sense of security she wants and needs. A man who travels a lot tells me, "I surprise the little woman with a phone call, flowers or a trinket when I'm out of town—just to let her know that "out of sight" is *not* "out of mind.""

"Diamonds are a girl's best friend" only if her husband forgets how she treasures his warm words and deeds of love. It's even possible that many women who buy fancy clothes do so in the hope of having their husbands say something nice. So cover your wife with your special kind of admiration, for which there is no substitute. Don't let a chance go by—say it.

Of course, admiration should work both ways. History is filled with stories of great romances inspired by women who were known not so much for their beauty as for their charm with words. Their secret? Knowing how to talk to a man, how to show they admired him.

During a lifetime devoted to answering questions about marriage, Dorothy Dix once commented on the reserve many women have in showing affection to their husbands. She said, "They say that flattery is okay for husbands, provided it is rationed. Maybe so, but keep in mind that with rationing there's usually a black market."

The private language gradually built up by the happy husband and wife heightens mutual admiration. They can't help reflecting in public the harmonious relationship they have in private. But if their "at-home" relationship is marked by dissension, their relationship in public will show it. The exposure of petty criticisms, contradictions and interruptions puts the couple at an added disadvantage. The more these aggressions are expressed—in voice, word and gesture—the more the husband and wife will lower each other's self-esteem and aggravate their difficulties.

A man who refers to himself as a "confirmed extrovert" recently remarked, "My daughter is going to marry a man who looks to me like an introvert—and I don't like the idea." In their excellent book *The Family*, E. W. Burgess and Harvey Locke point out that both outgoing (extrovert) and withdrawing (introvert) people have an equal chance at being happy or unhappy in marriage.

Those who like the company of other persons and those who dislike the company of other persons, those who do or who do not give a great deal of thought to the kind of impression they make upon others, and those who do or do not find it uncomfortable to be "different" are equally successful or unsuccessful in matrimony.

Burgess and Locke also discuss six psychological personality characteristics which can create unhappiness in marriage:

(1) an unhappy temperament, as indicated by a predisposition to be pessimistic rather than optimistic; (2) neurotic tendencies expressed by being touchy, grouchy, lonesome, easily hurt, and bothered by useless thoughts; (3) dominating and domineering behavior characterized by determination to get one's way and by disregard of the feelings of others; (4) critical and inconsiderate attitude toward others; (5) lack of self-confidence (on the part of the husband); and (6) self-sufficiency, as indicated by usually facing troubles alone and avoiding asking others' advice.

However, unhappiness in marriage, as well as happiness, results from the interaction of both personalities.

Just as no one can learn to ski without falling, so no marriage can exist without disagreement, perhaps even argument. The first lesson in skiing is learning how to fall without injury. By the same token, the first lesson in marriage is learning how to disagree, even argue, without being destructive.

A clipping sent by a friend in London, from an item by A. P. Herbert in the *News Chronicle*, makes good sense:

The concept of two people living together for 25 years without having a cross word suggests a lack of spirit only to be admired in sheep. When there is spirit there must be sparks.

The only hint I would offer on the subject of a happy marriage is, "Don't imagine that your first row will be the end of everything." It may be the end, but it's more likely to be the real beginning.

The only way to resolve difficulties is to give them an airing. If disagreements turn into arguments, keep them as brief as possible. Above all, don't let your temper trap you into saying things you'll regret.

Just recall the words of the happily married couple celebrating their golden anniversary who told news reporters they started marriage with a twenty-dollar gold piece and a maxim handed down from father to son: "Explain—explain—refrain from causing pain."

Stay clear of the chain of accusations, the backlog of past grievances that are hooked onto the incident that started the quarrel. The "I accuse" chain opens with statements like, "Six years ago you told me. . . ."

Talk about the deed, not the doer. Reflecting upon a lifetime of rich experience, Ethel Barrymore made as penetrating a statement about human relations as I have ever heard: "I suppose the greatest thing in the world is loving people and wanting to destroy the sin but not the sinner."

Family psychologists find that an attempt of one partner to dominate will often cause the other to feel threatened emotionally; naturally, difficulties and conflicts are the consequence. Only the mutual give-and-take that allows freedom in talking things over can bring satisfying answers to both. If the give-and-take is one-sided, the free channel of conversation is blocked by husband, wife, or both. For instance, they may not have enough interests in common, rarely be together, show little consideration for each other or not talk much.

R. S. Ort, in a study of conflicts in marriage, found that most of the happier couples settle disagreements by discussion.

When both husband and wife show a firm and lasting desire to talk it over, to help each other find a solution that both like, they can expect fewer disagreements and greater harmony. Most differences can be straightened out if a couple is willing to discuss them without anger, keeping their voices calm and talking slowly and deliberately.

Some hints on open discussion that can help make marriages happier are:
- A willingness to talk it over solves half the problem
- After you've thought it over, try to sense the right mood and time for talking it over. Sometimes the best time is now
- Use different approaches. Repeating the same words in the same way has less effect each time
- Be willing to consider a new point of view
- You don't have to be—no one can be—right all the time
- Compromise and understanding are the best insurance a marriage can have

Allow for a certain amount of frustration while trying to find a way. Some of the great men and women of wisdom have recognized that only those who are willing to fumble will reach their goals. After all, living is solving problems —and problems are solved first by talking and then by doing.

Be sure your talk is based on understanding, cooperation and collaboration—not competition. You can't be a good partner, either in marriage or in business while you're in business for yourself.

The values involved in happy marriage are very well summed up by Mrs. Eleanor Roosevelt:

In all human relationships, and marriage is one of the most difficult, I think perhaps the most important qualities of all individuals are unselfishness and flexibility. Tact can be a help also, and real love which occasionally carries you beyond interest in yourself is essential.

Conversation is the key to freedom of expression between husband and wife. As they become more capable in conversation, they will find it helps them create the deep confidence, true understanding and warm appreciation that make living complete.

Chapter Thirty-four

A GUIDE TO
PRESTIGE FOR
THE RISING EXECUTIVE

How much work can you do without talking to people? "Not much," you might say. "Maybe nothing at all!" The profit and loss of every business and profession depends entirely on talking and dealing with people—win, lose or draw.

If you should ask business, industrial and government leaders what their biggest and most important business is today, you would get three replies, but only one answer: "Human relations is our biggest business. We need people who know how to sell themselves and their ideas. We're always looking for leaders who know how to talk effectively." A perfectly correct answer, because most human relations operate through the channels of conversation.

Typical of many large corporations, the General Electric Company, employing about 250,000 people, is constantly in search of new managers, supervisors, foremen and other leadership personnel. In G.E., as in other companies, periodic appraisals of the managerial staff are made.

These evaluations are based on well over a hundred questions, including:

- Can people depend on what he says?
- Does he have courage to speak his mind against popular opinion when he is convinced he is right?
- Does he seek responsibility?
- Is he willing to admit that he may be wrong?
- Does he invite suggestions?
- Can he tactfully take issue with a point of view without antagonism?
- Does he encourage participation of others in his department?

The futures of many promising and some not-so-promising careers can be read when the answers come in. But the future of many careers can be predicted from the answer to only one of the many questions: "Can he talk and persuade?"

Some may be surprised to learn that a legal maxim states: "He who loses by his own negligence is not considered to have suffered any damage." But who will remind us that neglect of conversation skills can be damaging to our dealings with people?

As you recall the advances that you've made in your career, you'll find that they have come as a result of your increased ability to speak and deal with people. It's possible that your "know-how" in conversation was unknowingly based on the suggestions that follow. To review and confirm your ability, check yourself on the points that have helped many a man bridge the gap between an "also ran" and a top man.

ARE YOU FRIENDLY IN NAME ONLY?

You may always feel pinched for time in taking care of the many details that crowd your business day. But no matter how busy you are, before you start to circulate among the people in your firm, leave your problems on the desk—they'll be there when you get back. Leave yourself free to talk with people, to carry on good conversation relations. Look *at* people, not *through* them. Remember the simple amenities; say "hello" with a warm, friendly smile. The strange thing about some people is they never forget being ignored or overlooked, even if it's unintentional. Yet those same people will go to bat for you when the going is rough if they regard you as a nice, friendly guy.

"Me stop to chat? Can't be bothered. I'm too busy" is the brusque way a certain executive put it. I learned later of the unfortunate result of his attitude. When a crisis arose in his firm and *he* needed help, everyone else—by a not-so-curious coincidence—was "too busy." Taking the time to be friendly and "passing the praise around" have a way of paying hidden dividends and raising your rating.

DO YOU LISTEN WITH PATIENCE AND JUDGE WITH FAIRNESS?

Patient listening to the people you supervise is a "must" in business conversation. Listen objectively. Analyze the situation. Try very hard to be patient. Naturally you have to make some quick decisions. But try not to be pressured into taking a stand, especially if you haven't had time to think out a problem. Pressures always look more pressing up close. But from experience you know that one more calm minute or quiet hour will give you just enough time to review your decision. Wait, think about it, look at all the angles.

If you want people to give their best, remember how responsible and cooperative they become when they know they can depend on your fairness. Don't let prejudice make your decisions. Keep an open mind and be willing to revise your estimates of people—give them a break. Avoid judging hastily, even when under pressure.

If you were to ask five of your closest friends to describe the kind of person you are, you might be startled by the differences in their opinions. Since each of them is able to judge only through his own eyes, attitudes and experiences, there will be five opinions—all different.

Take a fresh and penetrating look at your boss—your associates—your right-hand man and girl Friday. Give people credit for having grown up. If possible, let them have the benefit of the doubt. The late Thomas J. Watson of I.B.M. once told me: "I judge a man by what he is and does today."

George Bernard Shaw, as usual, hit the target when he wrote: "The only man who behaves sensibly is my tailor. He takes my measure anew every time he sees me, whilst all the rest go on with their old measurements, and expect them to fit me."

ARE YOU BUILDING UP
YOUR "PERSUASION CREDIT"?

Would you ask to borrow a lawn mower from a neighbor you've never even spoken to? Maybe—but only if you were desperate. I'll bet you wouldn't make such a request unless you had already established friendly relations, or what I call "persuasion credit."

In a day and age when many of our profits are on paper and we trade on credit, personal relations must be kept on the credit side if management is to continue operating effectively. Through good conversation relations we can all build up our persuasion credit. The better our credit, the easier it is for us to persuade.

As we all know, if people believe in you, they will believe in what you say. It's the friend with whom you've established persuasion credit who will be there in a pinch.

On the other hand, poor persuasion credit is a luxury that some company executives—perhaps those who own the company—feel they can afford. They seem to forget that negative conversation relations result in resentment, and this turns up in red ink on the account books. How often have you overheard the low-voiced complaint, "He's throwing his weight around again?" Or how many employees may secretly retort with the now-famous knuckle-rapping line twanged out by Jane Ace: "You can't pull the bull over my eyes."

Some executives overlook the fact that the most persuasive executives are those who keep their authority under wraps. Naturally, it takes thought and energy to maintain a pleasant relationship throughout the business day, but it pays in many untold ways.

A former client, a successful self-made man, used to have the reputation of being overbearing and shouting at his executives and salesmen. One day he was shocked to find out that it was his brusque, bulldog behavior that was costing him his best men. They just wouldn't take it!

During our discussion I recalled the following words of another self-made man, Benjamin Franklin, who wrote in his *Autobiography*:

A Quaker friend having kindly informed me that I was generally thought proud; that my pride show'd itself frequently in conversation; that I was not content with being in the right when discussing any point, but was overbearing, and rather insolent, of which he convinced me by mentioning several instances; I determined endeavoring to cure myself, if I could, of this vice or folly.... I made it a rule to forbear all direct contradiction to the sentiments of others, and all positive assertion of my own.

Since this client was very profit-minded, he was willing to try a simple approach I recommended. He realized he would have to change the impression he made on people. First, he learned to soften his voice and speak without excitement. Then, beginning with one day a week, his only business of the day was to maintain friendly relations. He looked at his mail in the morning and spent the rest of the day circulating around the firm. After a while, he reported rather proudly that when others expected him to hit the roof, he surprised them by smiling and speaking quietly. He was even amused to catch a glimpse of the unbelieving looks that were exchanged. In time his new persuasion credit made his working relations both pleasant and profitable.

Getting a reputation for sincerity and thoughtfulness of others builds up a high persuasion credit. When you feel responsible for what you "sell," you will no longer have to persuade others. Instead, they will persuade you that what you are "selling" is right for them.

WHEN YOU COMMUNICATE DOES EVERYONE SEE THE SAME PICTURE?

Some years ago, on special assignment for Paramount Pictures, I had the privilege of working with the late Cecil B. DeMille. Together we worked out the scripts, and I then prepared Mr. DeMille for his radio broadcasts.

His great organizational ability was always apparent, and I expressed my admiration of the artistic composition of every scene in every one of his motion pictures. Mr. De-Mille then explained in simple terms the production techniques by which he achieved his supreme coordination of the lines of communication:

Yes, every picture is a frame of composition. Before we get on the set I consult with the artist staff and they draw many sketches of how the scenes are going to look on the motion picture screen. Then all my department heads receive copies of these sketches so that we all know what we're shooting for.

If, for instance, I were to tell you that a certain scene had to do with a barn in New Jersey, I might be thinking of a large, red barn ... while you might visualize a small barn that is practically in shambles ... someone else might see a picket fence around it ... and to another person, a barn in New Jersey might mean a brick stable for elegant race horses.

So that is why I have sketches made of every frame ... then there is no mistake about the scenery or the positions of the actors. And we all visualize the same artistic composition.

Producing a motion picture is big business, and it is a known fact that Mr. DeMille's scale of operation was *the* biggest.

In working with executives through the years I have found that the problems they face in communication are often a puzzle that makes them ask, in the words of Mr. DeMille, "Does everyone see the same picture?" Wherever you are in the chain of command and whatever your work, your promotions, profits and persuasive ability are supported on the same power lines as your ability to communicate. No doubt you have your own system of communication and feel quite confident about "getting through" with satisfactory results. But perhaps the basic suggestions that follow may give you a new look at that old problem—communication.

To communicate more clearly and accurately, try these suggestions: Reach the ears as well as the eyes! Don't stop after you've put it in writing—get it talked about, too. Sometimes it pays to repeat, and to repeat again: a basic principle of advertising. Notice in television commercials how often the key words are spoken by the announcer as they are simultaneously superimposed on the screen. And notice, too, how many times he repeats these key words.

Every time you assign work, take the time to explain clearly what is to be done; how it's to be done, if it's new and different; and when, in terms of total and "piece" goals—day, week, month.

Before a new routine is initiated, and also in troubleshooting, talk about it thoroughly with the people who are in charge of the work affected. A little advance talk may save lots of time, money and worry later. It even pays to review certain routines that may turn out to be trouble spots, talking them over "up and down the line." Pointed questions and thorough discussions can sometimes flash new light and insight on long-standing problems.

One business executive told me, "My greatest asset is that I can ask the right questions." Another way to say it is: "Leave the door open"—be available for all questions. Oddly enough, what appears at first to be a foolish question may point directly at the weak spot in a communications system.

Always follow up. Keep records of progress and watch results. Fix responsibility for work, and for having it proceed according to agreement or contract. Make periodic checks with people responsible. And don't overlook the value of giving credit where credit is due. A few well-chosen words are the biggest stimulant to continuing good work—and are not automatically thought of as an invitation to ask for a raise.

Be absolutely sure that everyone on your team understands precisely what you want him to do. If it's especially important, agree on procedure, establish priorities. Finally, if there's any question about the message getting across, even after you've spelled it out, "draw the pictures" that will make it crystal clear.

ARE YOU SILENT WHEN YOU SHOULD BE TALKING?

The active part-owner of a manufacturing company explained why he had the reputation of being the "silent partner." Associated for years with a man who took the dominant role in representing the firm and selling its products, our "silent partner" had long since grown used to taking the back seat. Lately he has become more uncomfortable when he must talk—and now finds it quite difficult to participate in meetings. The "talking" partner has taken to chiding him on his silence, and the other day is reported to have said brashly, "It's all right to be silent, Joe, but you're making a career out of it." That's when Joe decided to do something about it.

Unfortunately, many people try to solve their original discomfort in talking by letting others who are willing take over. Since ease in talking increases with experience, the habitually silent person who must speak in a business conference is likely to find himself at a decided disadvantage. He probably feels as shaky as the man who—not having skied for many years—suddenly finds himself atop the toughest ski run. Frequent silences lead to misunderstanding and reduce a person's effectiveness in dealing with others.

Silence, properly used, can be a decided advantage—and often is the most dynamic "statement" anyone can make. Silence can be a plus to any person who is capable of saying what he means, of standing his ground with poise and confidence.

As the president of a large San Francisco department store once told me, "If you never fail in business, you will never grow rich." Silence is golden only if you are not afraid to talk—and if you know how and when to talk.

CAN YOU KEEP AN ARGUMENT UNDER CONTROL?

Many important business conferences and conversations have been disrupted because no one knew how to keep a flash of temper from short-circuiting the business at hand. Once tempers pyramid and voices shout in argument, the "fat's in the fire"; reason gives way to antagonistic feelings. Words spoken in anger are later regretted and sometimes leave scars that are never forgotten. How, then, can the efficient executive prepare to control possible disagreements and restore harmonious relations?

Stuart Chase in *The Tyranny of Words* describes a technique he has found successful in preventing arguments.

The essence is in *listening*. Don't hit, don't contradict, don't cave in or turn the other cheek. Just say: "Tell me some more, I'm listening!"

If you refuse to get angry, your antagonizer will simmer down. If you can control your feelings, remain quiet and listen, you will eventually extinguish the flare-up of temper. Keep your listening passive if you want it to be effective.

Once during a Hollywood story conference a producer, who was instructing his director, stopped abruptly and said, "What do you mean by arguing with me?" The director looked puzzled. "I haven't said a word!" "Well," complained the producer, "you were listening in a very aggressive manner."

The supreme test for self-mastery during arguments is the ability to summarize what the other person has said. Keep busy trying to understand the major points and reasons without jumping to any conclusions.

Should you be disturbed by a chronic arguer, follow these tested and proven suggestions of James F. Sirmons, Assistant Director of Labor Relations for the Columbia Broadcasting System. Having great respect for his ability, I asked Mr. Sirmons to tell me about some of the methods he has found valuable. He said:

Losing your temper immediately puts you at the mercy of others. We lose our tempers because we take something that was said personally. When you begin to feel the sensations of anger, change the pace. Look at your notes—whisper to others on your team, if you can—even take out your handkerchief and

blow your nose. Then, if possible, come back to a different
question.

Instead of calling the man who irritated you an idiot, ask him
a question about what he said. Repeat in your own words what
you believe he said, and ask if you understood him correctly.
Shift the emphasis from the person to the idea or issue. Instead of hinting that the person is at fault, question the value
of his statement. Tell why you think it won't work—and, if
you can, give your own idea in a way to meet the problem.

Those who think others may call them a weakling if
they don't argue and raise their voices can take a tip from
Rocky Graziano, the former middleweight champion of
the world. His remedy, he tells me, is simply this: "When
a guy gets hot under the collar...I walk away. I don't
look for trouble. I do all my fightin' in the ring." People
who know their own power know there's nothing to be
gained from throwing their weight around.

If you can get rid of the muscle tension that anger causes,
you can increase your control over yourself and also over
the situation. When you feel tension, try to lean back
in your chair. Tense your muscles, and then release to relax them. Breathe slowly and deeply. And control your
desire to speak!

By the time the arguer has had his say, you will be in
a better condition to control the situation. Some "tranquil-
izing" statements to put an argument on ice can be of
service if you speak them quietly, slowly, while gently
nodding your head to show you understand. Try these:

"I see what you mean."
"You've brought up a very important point."
"Yes, that's right."
"When I get a chance, I'd like to look it up." And if
you run out of dialogue, just keep saying, "Yeh-ah-hah ...
hmm-uh-huh."

Remember that arguments grow when one person tries to top another. If you can keep it from becoming a "Can You Top This," you'll have a good start at controlling—and cooling off—the argument. Before long you'll be able to spot the clouds before the storm, and then you'll run up a good record for maintaining harmony in conference and conversation.

Chapter Thirty-five

TO BE THE
HOST AND HOSTESS
WITH THE MOSTEST

Every time you have a party you become a sort of "conversation manager." The best entertainment you can give your friends after a warm greeting is to arrange and stimulate informative, interesting and exciting conversation.

Introduce each guest with a proud smile and pronounce the name with respect. Ring out each name nice and clear; they'll love you for it. Give the names importance, and pause slightly after each one.

If the name is new and you're not sure of it, ask in pleasant tones, "How do you spell it?" or "Did I pronounce your name right?" If possible, you might have something warm or interesting to say about the name or add: "Harry told me a lot about you," "I've been wanting to meet you" or "I'm glad you finally made it."

Let's try a round of introductions for a couple just joining the group (pause one or two seconds at each line mark):

"I'd like you all to meet (*or* May I introduce) Mr. and Mrs. Stanton/—Dick and Harriet./Harriet and Dick, I'd like you to meet/Alice and John Boomer,/Philip Jensen,/Marie Cowan,/Harriet and Dick Stanton." (Repeat as you move on to the next group.) If a guest—man or woman —is a judge, other official, professor or doctor, use the title unless you're asked to do otherwise.

Nobody intentionally mumbles, slurs, or mispronounces a name. But if you make a mistake, don't be ashamed to try again. Say, "Oh, I'm sorry . . ." and carry on. (Jokes with names are not good form.)

While I was visiting the Raymond Masseys, Mrs. Massey told me with a smile how her husband had a way of mumbling introductions. Every guest he introduced seemed to be named something like "M-a-m-o-u-l-i-a-n." At one party, becoming exasperated with this gentle mumbling, she leaned toward the man who had just been introduced, saying: "I didn't hear Ray; what is your name?" The gentleman answered, "My name is Mamoulian."

"Mamoulian! But it can't be, I. . . ."

"Always has been," he said, giving her a puzzled look, "Rouben Mamoulian."

As you introduce and later circulate among your guests, seeing to their comfort and pleasure, you may already be focusing the spotlight on them, as many clever hosts do.

John Shaheen, public relations expert and radio-TV station owner, will introduce a doctor friend with a dramatic bit of information like, "I'd like you to meet the man who saved my life. Last time we went hunting I got some splinters in my face. Doc, here, took them out so skillfully there are no marks."

John will turn to an attorney friend and say, "Now Jack, there, is the best lawyer in town." These "verbal medals" will usually bring satisfied smiles and chipper comments all around. Try it yourself and watch the glow on people's faces.

Clients will ask, "How can I start the conversation ball rolling?" I tell them that drawing people out is one good way to spread good feeling all around. In launching your friends with "send off" words that frame them with interest, you'll be doing for them what they could never do for themselves.

If a guest is an insurance broker, you might say, "Well, Harry, I hear you wrapped up a big deal last week—insuring Jimmy Durante's nose for a million dollars!" You could ask Hy, an investor, "What's your opinion of the market these days?" Hy can talk about this topic or his hobby, whichever you bring up. Either topic will make him look good. The more specific or amusing the better. To another guest you might say, "How's your football-playing son?" or "How's that beautiful garden? I don't know how you can take care of your family and keep up with that big garden, too."

Bits of information like these start an exchange among the guests and help them to talk and get acquainted. You make it possible for them to avoid the labored "Who are you—what do you do?" quiz and the embarrassment that comes from saying the wrong thing to the wrong person ("Should I tell John the man he's been talking to for the past forty minutes is not the president of The Paconic Company?").

The more we know about people the more interesting we are likely to find them. As our interest in them increases, they naturally become more interested in us, too.

Differences of opinion can be stimulating, if they're kept on a good-humored level. If a discussion causes a guest to get edgy, a well-timed interruption and a relaxed comment by the host or hostess can restore ease and change the subject. The good host or hostess first reassures the person who is most excited—then, if necessary, tactfully clarifies the situation.

The successful party is an occasion when the guests feel free to express themselves, but without making anyone uncomfortable. And it's the host or hostess who encourages this feeling of freedom. But don't overburden yourself by feeling responsible for more than is reasonable, for turning a "strong silent man" into a talker or a wall flower into the "belle of the ball."

The interaction of personalities in the group, as well as the influence of the host and hostess, sets the mood of any party. You've probably found some gatherings a little too "starchy" for comfort. And also some that got wildly out of hand. Are the people at your party entertaining to each other? That's the important thing, isn't it?

The most interesting conversations rise in pitch and tempo when there are one or two stimulating participants. For instance, if you happened to meet Victor Hammer, art dealer and raconteur, you couldn't help enjoying his animated talk. He loves to laugh and exchange anecdotes and is equally at home with Salvador Dali or a roomful of cowpokes.

Dorothy Gordon, moderator of *The New York Times* Youth Forum (NBC-TV), a stimulating listener and truly vital when talking, loves to introduce people who "will like each other."

Another example of vitality is Mr. Justice Felix Frankfurter. Archibald MacLeish tells a story of a Sunday morning breakfast at a friend's big house in Virginia. "There were about thirty guests and the talk was loud—so loud that Frankfurter's clerk apologized for it. 'Jedge, is there too much noise to suit you?'

" 'Too much noise!' snorted the Justice. 'How could there be too much noise? Have you ever heard me complaining about too much noise?'

" 'No, Jedge! But Jedge—this is the other feller's noise!'

"Now, Justice Frankfurter," continues Archibald MacLeish, "loves the touch of people. He stands near them when he talks, catching them by the arm. He turns the talk of two or three at one end of a self-conscious dinner

table into a drama of the whole table, in which self-consciousness is lost. He moves quickly and precisely from
one place to another in a crowded room, and suddenly the
room is drawn together. He shouts with laughter in the
stilted, formal silence. And the silence comes alive."

Your best bet, whether host or guest, is to favor others
without competing with anyone, and to be your best self.
The people who don't strain make the best impressions.

Singing star Risë Stevens, in a *Reader's Digest* article,
writes how she suffered from social embarrassment:

> For years I had been a nervous hostess. . . .
> My discomfort, I found, came from trying to be something
> I was not—a star in the drawing room as well as on stage. If a
> clever person made a joke, I tried to top it—and failed. I pre-
> tended to be familiar with subjects I knew nothing of. . . .
> Facing my faults, I began listening and asking questions at
> parties instead of trying to impress the guests. I discovered
> that I had much to learn from others. When I spoke, I tried
> to contribute, not to shine. . . .

Once Risë Stevens had learned to trust her real self,
she could stop pretending. Her reward—a new and complete joy in being with people. People always prefer the
real you.

When we accept ourselves as we are, we can then accept
others as they are. In my lectures one point that I stress
about conversation relations is: "We are never so dis-
enchanted with others as when we are dissatisfied with
ourselves." When we are sincere and friendly, nine times
out of ten people will reflect our feelings. Mark Twain, a
great observer of people, said of a popular friend: "He
liked to like people, therefore people liked him."

Whether you are President of the United States or a
Good Humor man, whether you're guest or host, you can't
please everyone all the time—including yourself. Forgive
others their human frailties—we all have them.

After you've done all you can to make the party fun for your guests, don't worry about the details—enjoy your party. When you've done your best, never worry about what "they" will say.

Elsa Maxwell, society columnist and famous hostess, describes one of the rules left her as a "legacy" by her father. "Never be afraid of 'they,' " he told her.

"Who is 'they'?" Elsa inquired.

"You, him, it, me—anybody," he answered. "People are more afraid of 'they' than anything else in the world. Strong generals with great armies will face courageously the most outrageous foes yet be terrified of what 'they' might say, 'they' might do, 'they' mightn't like." Elsa's supreme confidence as a hostess certainly recommends this rule to all of us.

Speaking of the greatest and most enjoyable sport, the late William Allen White once remarked, "The best thing in the world from the standpoint of human satisfaction is to talk . . . good talk is worth all it costs." And where else can good talk be so good as at a party?

Chapter Thirty-six

DO YOU MAKE
THESE MISTAKES
IN CONVERSATION?

The tricky curves in conversation traffic should be handled with care. Sometimes the most rapid improvements in conversation are made by knowing what *not* to do.

DO YOU INTERRUPT AT
THE WRONG TIME?

A Hollywood writer was telling me about a friend of his I had met once: "You know, Dick has a speech impediment."

"I hadn't noticed. What is it?" I asked.

"Well," he replied, with a twinkle in his eye, "every time he opens his mouth his wife interrupts."

Many people are forever interrupting; they can't allow anyone to finish a sentence. The compulsion to break in while someone else is talking can fracture the friendly flow of conversation. Some people not only interrupt, they completely change the subject, making a U turn in the conversation.

At a party some years ago I noticed the late Fred Allen puckishly snipping the air with a pair of scissors. "Tonight I'm a conversation snipper," he explained. "I'm just doing what everyone else here is doing—snipping off the ends of

206

sentences that others are saying, just to put in their own
—which are always *non sequitur*'s. And nothing is relevant
to anything that has been said or will be said."

What was Fred Allen talking about? Let's listen to two
married couples spending an evening together.

Husband 1:   There we were, in the middle of nowhere
             at 4:00 a.m. when . . .

Wife 1:   I think it was only a little after two, dear.
             I remember . . .

Husband 1:   Yeah, well maybe it was two. So, no gas
             . . . not another car in . . .

Wife 1:   The kids were hungry, too. I knew we
             should have stayed in Auburn . . .

Husband 1:   Yeah, well, okay, I . . .

Wife 1:   But you know Mike . . .

Wife 2:   We had an awful time when . . .

Husband 2:   Yeah, in Canada. It was snowing like . . .

Wife 2:   I thought I'd never . . .

Husband 2:   Wow! What a time we had!

Wife 2:   We should have gone to . . .

(*Now all four talk at once*)

Husband 2:   Imagine, there was the Chateau Fronte-
             nac up on . . .

Wife 2:   It's just like I was saying to Mary the
             other day . . .

Wife 1:   Well, as long as you end up safe and
             sound it really . . .

Husband 1:   Who's at the wheel, that's . . . that's what
             counts when you've got bad weather . . .

And that's how it is with people who frequently interrupt
one another. Notice that most abrupt interruptions are
about minor details and that sooner or later interrupters
are themselves interrupted and frequently end up talking
at the same time.

If you feel that your conversation relations would improve if you interrupted less, you may find the techniques suggested here helpful. First, be aware of your body position. As soon as you start leaning forward, as if getting ready to dive in, that's the time to put the brakes on. Take a deep breath and lean all the way back. If you can make yourself lean back, you've won half the battle. Relaxing and getting the most out of listening and observing will decrease your desire to cut in.

If interrupting is a long-standing problem, you may find more dramatic measures in order. With mouth closed, place the tip of your tongue between your teeth and press gently—without making it obvious. I know this sounds amusing, but it gets good results. Try to hold your tongue there for about a minute. Then release it and speak—for about half a minute. Say only as much as you can say in this time; then give others a chance to talk. If they don't (give them time), then go on talking.

Keep repeating the closed-mouth routine for about five minutes at a time—and whenever necessary.

DO YOU CONTRADICT?

Contradicting others is one of the easiest and fastest ways to lose friends and make enemies. Not even a man's wife or best friend can stand the strain of a flat contradiction.

"No! You are mistaken, I'm sure," a handsome woman I know is in the habit of saying. She speaks rapidly in a high-pitched voice, which adds harshness to her caustic remarks. Yes, she has the facts to prove she is right, and she cannot resist putting another person in the wrong. One of her former friends who has felt her sting once said of her, "She could do better if she threw a stone into a hornets' nest."

Benjamin Franklin was a master at persuading others to

do what he believed was right. His method, explained in his *Autobiography*, is worth recalling: "I made it a rule to forebear all direct contradiction to the sentiments of others, and all positive assertion of my own...."

ARE YOU BRUTALLY FRANK?

Another way to damage conversation relations is to insist on being brutally frank at all times. Far from getting a reputation for honesty, people who are brutally frank—who have a compulsion to call a fig a fig—succeed only in offending everyone present. They never stop to ask themselves: "Is what I am saying true? And if it's true, is it necessary? Even if it's true, will it do any good? Or is it cruel, perhaps destructive?" What these people say is always—yes, always—resented, and they invariably harm themselves more than others.

The point is dramatized by a piercing remark once made by portrait painter John Singer Sargent: "Every time I paint a portrait, I lose a friend."

Frankness and honesty are essential to good human relations. But there is a time and place—and always a kind way—that makes the point without the pain.

DO YOUR STATEMENTS
"CLOSE THE DOOR"?

Every time you give your opinion in a distinctly emphatic way—making statements in words, voice or gesture that close the door—you are interfering with the free flow of good conversation. Believe it or not, even facts can be as useless as a hole in a pail unless they are properly presented.

If you want people to respect your opinion, avoid making flat, firm statements and all-inclusive or all-exclusive pronouncements. And if you make a mistake, admit it—but not grudgingly. Let the other person get a kick out of your telling him he was right. The evidence you have will be more quickly and fully accepted—even by the most insecure people—if you offer it quietly and with humility. Overpositive statements cause most people to feel inferior. And in trying to save their own self-respect, they may lose respect for you.

The late drama critic George Jean Nathan once remarked, "No woman who speaks emphatically can be lovely." An insight just as valid for men as for women.

DO YOU TALK ABOUT YOURSELF TOO MUCH?

The person who talks on and on about himself is—except on rare occasions—exasperating and even offensive. Most of us can benefit from cutting down the number of times we say "I, me, my, mine" and increasing our use of "you" and "your" in our conversation.

We can better appreciate the effect that talking too much about ourselves may have on other people and understand their resentment if we keep in mind Addison Mizener's target-hitting tip: "Don't talk about yourself; it will be done when you leave."

DO YOU HAND OUT ADVICE?

If you are a professional person, it's your job to give advice on subjects within your specialty. That's why people seek you out. If you're not in a profession whose purpose is to give information and advice, keep in mind that unasked-for advice is always in poor taste, usually useless and sometimes humiliating. If, on occasion, you can't avoid giving advice, dole it out with a teaspoon—not a ladle.

The person who goes out of his way to give advice should recognize that it is not always a satisfying experience for those who receive the advice. Advice, rarely appreciated, is often resented. Lord Chesterfield made the point perfectly in these words: "Advice is seldom welcomed; and those who want it the most always like it the least."

ARE YOU OVERLY SARCASTIC?

Many forced attempts to be amusing or provocative produce sarcasm and may offend our listeners. Sarcasm—more frequent among men—is a form of "sociable aggression" that is prevalent in country-club locker rooms, lunch rooms and bars—wherever men gather. Most sarcasm is not just innocent fun—it's camouflaged criticism. Starting salty, it soon turns bitter. Some barb-throwing camaraderie is expected to bring laughter—the forced "jolly good fellow" kind of laughter.

Because no one wants to be pointed out as a poor sport, few complain or seem to show they "can't take it." But reactions do come. A man will either jab back with his own brand of banter or build up a grudge against "that character" who persists in piercing his ego. Some men honestly don't enjoy this type of kidding. Others only enjoy it when they can hit back twice as hard.

The "social comedian" whose barbs spare no one's feelings is a pest. He may have his day but sooner or later winds up on the unwelcome-guest list. Just as unpopular is the sarcastic cynic with the "sour grapes" attitude, who makes others feel uncomfortable. From novelist Fanny Hurst comes this sage remark: "It takes a clever man to turn cynic and a wise man to be clever enough not to."

Whatever the method—attempting to cut the other fellow down is only a brash way of trying to overcome one's own feelings of inferiority. Usually it's a give-away that the sarcastic person is actually envious of the very person he is needling.

Most people are far more sensitive than they appear to be. Sarcasm, like other forms of humor, can be very funny

under certain conditions. The best conditions are in theatrical productions, and the next best when there is tre-
mendous brotherly love. But when the intent is aggressive,
to persist in "digging into someone," in any way to hu-
miliate or challenge his self-esteem—conversation is then
used as a weapon. So in "kidding around with the boys,"
keep it on the "playing field of fair play." And—most important—know when to stop!

Chapter Thirty-seven

WHAT DO PEOPLE
SAY ABOUT YOU?

The president of an advertising agency, who had called me in on a special problem, revealed the cause of his concern in these words: "During the past few months we've lost 25 per cent of our billing—and all of it new accounts," he said. "I've talked to some of my boys and haven't been able to get much information. And, confidentially," continued the president, leaning forward, "last week I talked to one of our old clients, and from what he told me, I've an idea we lose out during campaign proposals. That," the president added, "is what I want you to do—help me figure out what's going wrong in those meetings."

After discussing the matter, we decided—with the agreement of the executives involved—to record samples of several such meetings. It is interesting to note that in the interplay of conference and conversation, even though people know what they're saying is being recorded, they soon relax and talk as they do naturally. And that's all we need to help them improve their conversation techniques.

The playback supplied the answer to the lost accounts. The oldest member of the agency, an account executive referred to as "Mr. Senior," dominated all the talk on the tapes. Blustery and overbearing, he took advantage of his seniority rights. The president was shocked to hear him veto every suggestion from the other executives. "Mr. Senior" showed a generally negative attitude, and his repeated contradictions obviously irritated the clients. Turning to me, the president exclaimed, "I don't know what's happened to Bill! If I were a client, I wouldn't do business with him, either."

The agency president gave "Mr. Senior," a stockholder in the company, a different but equally important supervisory position—without client contact. During the consultations that followed, the executives and I worked on their conference techniques—another way of saying conversation relations.

This advertising agency had a problem that involved business, but the business of our conversation relations goes on every waking hour, every time we talk or deal with people. If you recorded your everyday conversations, what would your reaction be to what you heard? A happy surprise? Or just surprise?

If we listened to our conversations and thought about them, we could discover many new things about ourselves. The "inside information" we'd get from analyzing these recordings could be put to good use in improving our relations with others. "Fine idea," you might be thinking, "but very impractical."

Not so impractical, however. For some time I have had sales and business clients record samples of their "conversation in action." I analyze the recordings—both business conversation and sales pitch. Then, after discussing the trouble spots, we devise new techniques to refine and strengthen the conversation techniques of the client— whether business interview, conference or sales pitch.

People are often intrigued by what others say about them

when they're not there. It's natural for people to talk about others—we all do it. What do you think people say about you? Maybe they're saying something that could be useful to you: "I wish she'd stop talking about herself all the time" or "Poor guy—always complaining" or "Why does he argue so much?" or "If you can get a word in edgewise when she's around, you're lucky." Then again, perhaps your conversation rating is high, and people are saying some very nice things about you.

Since we express our total personality through our conversation, it follows that our faults as well as our positive qualities are revealed every time we speak. Certain difficulties in conversation derive from our opinions and attitudes, and we can improve our conversation—after we have changed our attitudes. Perhaps the first thing we need to do is to accept our faults—to make peace with them. As La Rochefoucauld observed: "Almost all our faults are more pardonable than the methods we think up to hide them."

Rudyard Kipling once pointed out, "If you hit a pony over the nose at the outset of your acquaintance, he may not love you, but he will take a deep interest in your movements ever afterwards." Like the pony, many of us have lived through similar "growing pain" lessons in conversation. Yes, we have learned the hard way! Lucky for us we don't have to keep going to the "school of disillusionment." We can get a transfer.

Anyone can transfer to the "school of know-how." This school is open to us once we accept ourselves and have a willingness to appreciate others. As we refuse to be wrapped up in ourselves or make snap judgments about people, we will notice that our conversation relations improve. A graduate of the "school of know-how" is the person Mrs. Eleanor Roosevelt is speaking of when she says:

A mature person is one who does not think only in absolutes, who is able to be objective even when deeply stirred emotionally, who has learned that there is both good and bad in all people and all things, and who walks humbly and deals charitably with the circumstances of life, knowing that in this world no one is all-knowing and therefore all of us need both love and charity.

And what is love? What is charity? Do not both grow out of a genuine interest in others? There can be no genuine interest in others until we have true respect for ourselves. Then, and only then, will our positive qualities shine through when we speak—and we can take pleasure in what others are saying about us.

Chapter Thirty-eight

CONVERSATION
IN ACTION

The improvement sessions that follow are a new collection of practical and entertaining ideas to sharpen your conversation. Here you will have a chance to speak freely and observe other people's reactions while making adjustments to increase your own skill. These sessions will build up your ability to think and speak with confidence and influence. The more care you take in planning each session and the more you try to outdo yourself, the better the results.

Form a regular group of four or more (ten is good). Work with a good tape recorder, if you can, and keep some of the tape reels for comparison with later sessions.

⸕ TV DISCUSSION

Select a topic—choose a guest authority, a moderator and four panel members. Let the discussion follow the established pattern, the guest authority answering questions posed by panel members and moderator. Follow the outline of unrehearsed programs like *The New York Times* Youth Forum (NBC-TV). Dorothy Gordon, moderator-producer of the program, described the pre-broadcast activities to me: "I meet the young panelists for the first time shortly before we go on the air. They are prepared to discuss our weekly topic, but I never know what they're going to say. The comments of our guest expert are also spontaneous."

Each member of your group will profit from taking his turn acting as moderator, guest expert and panelist. The topics should allow for conflicting opinions—they make for more lively talk. Choose your topic well in advance so that all can come prepared. (*The New York Times* discussion outlines can be of service.)

TV COLUMN

Assign columns or sections on different topics that have been clipped out of a newspaper or magazine to each member of the group: fashion, politics, family, finance, cooking, travel, sports, medicine. Each person studies the assigned column and reports on it to the group—speaking as the expert columnist.

After the "column" has been "broadcast," the "guest columnist" is questioned by the group. For example: "You said in your column that there will be a new trend in our economy—on what do you base your opinion?" or "Why do you believe fashions will not change drastically next year?"

NEWS REPORT

Each member makes a study of the latest news from a different part of the world, as reported in the previous Sunday's edition. Consulting brief notes, he begins his news report to the group by saying, for example: "This is John Rumley reporting from London. . . ." The report finished, the reporter is questioned by the person who has earlier been assigned the role of "anchor man."

PERSONAL INTERVIEW

Members are assigned roles of various prominent people. Each might be allowed only ten minutes—or ten days —to plan what he will say. Some may wish to do a little research and study (news reports, articles and speeches). The interviewer is allowed three to ten minutes to ask the questions he's prepared. It may go like this: "Mr. _____, I understand you've been appointed the new Commissioner of Motor Vehicles. What do you intend to do about safer driving?" or "Senator _____, we understand that you've been working for the _____ Bill. How will it benefit farmers?" or "Madame Ambassador, what can the American tourist do to encourage friendliness?" or "Mr. _____, if you're elected governor, what will be your first order of business?"

IN MY OPINION...

Collect published speeches made by the President, your Governor, Senators, Representatives, Mayor and other well-known people. You can find these in newspapers and in special publications like *Vital Speeches*. Assign delivery of a speech to each person ("Joe, you're the Governor, and you made this talk last week."). Joe then studies the talk, underlines the important points and makes helpful notes. After his speech, he is interviewed by another member who acts the part of a newspaper reporter.

BOARD MEETING

Each member is given a company title: chairman, president, vice-president, secretary, treasurer, research and development director, production manager, personnel manager, chief engineer, etc. The chairman leads the discussion on topics that involve company planning, profits, new developments, and other matters. For example: "Should the

B plant be moved to another state—and why?" or "How can we increase production?" or "How can we improve our public relations?" or "How can we improve employee relations?" Each member of the group should be ready with a report. He also should be able to answer questions on his report.

HOLLYWOOD STORY LINE

Each member speaks for about one to three minutes (use a stop watch). The first makes up a scenario of a motion picture and the others narrate additions to the plot, developing and adding characters and changing the scene along the way. For instance, the start could be: "This picture is located in the harbor area of San Francisco. The leading characters are a freight loader; his sister, who is a school teacher; and a woman who teaches in the same school she does. The story begins in a cheap boarding house. The guests are eating dinner when they hear a scream and two shots." When time is up, or when each person runs out of material, the next member takes it from there, adding to the story line. When the story has run its course, a lively conversation follows. Is our hero sympathetic? Should the heroine really adopt the child? How about the ending—is it strong enough?

CAN YOU TOP THIS?

Each member tells an anecdote or story on a topic chosen the previous week: fishing, selling, children, tramps, farmers, parties.

The story that gets the best reaction is rated as the "topper"—a prize always adds to the fun. Each listener makes brief (anonymous) notes suggesting how the joke or anecdote could have been improved in the telling or the material. If time permits, the speaker can, after reading the comments, retell the story.

Part Six

SPEAK IN PUBLIC WITH NEW CONFIDENCE

Chapter Thirty-nine

THE SHORT CUT
TO RECOGNITION

If you were suddenly singled out of a group and asked to make an informal luncheon talk, or if you were chosen to speak at a business meeting, or even to broadcast to millions of people over radio and television—how would you sound to your listeners?

Reporting on his first talk, at a luncheon in Los Angeles, a former client wrote:

> When I got up to speak I felt a little tense at first but relaxed as soon as I had the audience with me. They seemed to like what I said and how I said it. When I finished I couldn't believe all the applause was for me. Later some of the boys came up to congratulate me and wanted to know why they hadn't seen me around. All I said was, "I've been here all along."

Some men and women speak in public to receive recognition, some because it's part of their work. But most people who speak well in public do so because they "got the message" a long time ago. *Good public speaking is the shortest route to becoming well-known in your own company or community.*

S. C. Allyn, chairman of National Cash Register, a com-

pany famous for its sales methods, expressed the sentiments
of hundreds of company presidents throughout the United
States when he wrote about "Speech and Leadership in
Business" in the *Quarterly Journal of Speech:*

... no man can expect to achieve maximum success in our
selling organization without the ability to speak well in public.
And I think the same can be said of salesmen of any other company. [The National Cash Register Company employs over two
thousand salesmen.]

... in the history of our business, many a man has drawn
attention to himself by a good job done on the platform.... A
good many years ago a young man who was then in charge of a
small NCR branch in Kansas ... gave a rather unusual talk ...
and is, today, our vice-president in charge of sales.

Your wish may be simple—just to say a few well-chosen
words in a calm voice. Or perhaps you'd like to have more
confidence when you're selling yourself in business dealings, meetings and conferences. You may even have a secret
dream of delivering an important speech. Speaking in
public while others listen with attention, respect and interest may still be one of your unfulfilled desires.

If you have never given yourself a chance to develop
your speaking abilities, the time may be now. If you apply
these easy-to-follow and practical methods that have
worked so well for others, you can soon be on your way to
winning applause for your public speaking.

Chapter Forty

YOUR KEY TO
CONFIDENCE—
PREPARE WITH CARE

Your plane is moving into position for take-off. Suddenly you ask yourself: "Did they fill the tanks? Did they check the engines?" What foolish questions!

Of course they did! You don't doubt for a moment that everything was done. If you did, you wouldn't be sitting in that plane. You're positive all necessary preparations were made. Then why, tell me, do people rise to speak— carelessly prepared?

Just as the plane is thoroughly checked, so your "journey into public speaking" depends on careful preparation. And it's this preparation that is your insurance against a "never-got-off-the-ground" rating. When you prepare with care, your "flight chart" will read: "lifted the audience—airtight message smoothly delivered—mission accomplished."

Lloyd George, a former Prime Minister of Britain recognized for his ability as a public speaker, wisely observed:

To trust to the inspiration of the moment—that is the fatal phrase upon which many promising careers have been wrecked. The surest road to inspiration is preparation. I have seen many men of courage and capacity fail for lack of industry. Mastery in speech can only be reached by mastery in one's subject.

225

If you want to save time in planning and delivering a successful talk, learn to look up information and pick up some hints on writing. When a man apologizes for not having had a college education, I ask him, "Do you know where to find the material you need? Can you research and write up a problem?" If you can say "yes" to this question —whatever your formal education—you are better off than many college graduates.

Set up a base of good speaking operations. Visit your library often enough to cash in on the vast vault of information that is available to you. For ideas and inspiration, for improving your wealth and welfare, "look it up."

Many good books on writing are available. Perhaps you've read some of them. If you have little time to spare you may want to look into Stephen Leacock's *How to Write*, especially if you want to be amused while learning. You'll find some practical suggestions, too, in Rudolph Flesch's *The Art of Readable Writing*.

Better speaking, as well as good writing, is built on the ability to put ideas into words, to create pictures that make others see and feel. That's why the letters that get the most action are the letters that "talk to you."

Let's say you're planning to give a brief talk and you've chosen your topic. You've collected illustrations and anecdotes and completed your research. Now you are ready to make an outline. Even though you will make several points in your talk, they ought to add up to one major point. That major point should be so definite that even if your audience forgets everything else, they'll remember that one point. That's the best that most speakers can hope for. As you begin to develop your talk from your outline, you will continue to make changes in both the outline and the talk.

Unless speakers are very experienced, I always suggest the talk be written out completely. Writing out your talk will spark many other ideas and help you recall the interesting experiences and illustrations that will make your talk come alive. Once your talk is on paper, think about it, sleep on it, try to visualize and mull over the dramatic images that will appeal to your audience.

Dr. Charles R. Brown, Dean of the Yale Divinity School for many years, describes in *The Art of Preaching* the method he found effective in preparing lectures:

Brood over your text and your topic. Brood over them until they become mellow and responsive. You will hatch out of them a whole flock of promising ideas as you cause the tiny germs of life there contained to expand and develop....

Keep on putting down all the ideas which come to your mind, thinking hard all the while. You need not hurry this process. It is one of the most important mental transactions in which you will be privileged to engage. It is this method which causes the mind to grow in real productive power....

Through the ages the finest speakers and performers have followed one rule: they *live* preparation. Would you like to know how Paul Muni, one of the greatest living character actors of our time, prepares a role? For months before shooting ever started on *The Life of Pasteur*, Muni ate and slept the role of Dr. Pasteur—getting ready for his portrayal of that great scientist. What clothes did Pasteur wear? In what pocket did he carry his watch? How did Dr. Pasteur eat his soup? How did he carry his cane?

Muni studied and lived his characterization, gradually building his portrayal into a "living" Dr. Pasteur. When he finally went before the cameras, the results of his advance work were evident in every scene—and the role is one of the most memorable performances of Muni's entire career.

It is surprising to note that at a time when great orators were in fashion, Abraham Lincoln was not considered an "orator." He spoke intimately—as he would if broadcasting over television today. His fame grew and spread, but why—when he did not conform to the speaking style of his day? Because in his homespun way he would tell an amusing anecdote to illustrate his point—that was his charm and power. He created pictures that people would remember. The strength of Lincoln's speeches was in his imaginative thinking.

Abraham Lincoln searched for knowledge at a time when it was not nearly so accessible as it is to us today. Emil Ludwig, in his biography of Lincoln, writes:

One day a customer brings him tidings of an English grammar, at a farm six miles away. He walks over to borrow the book, and for the first time becomes acquainted with the systematization of his own language. An acquaintance lends him a volume of Gibbon; from the minister he gets another history book; he learns much from talks with the schoolmaster, and from questioning things and people.

Lincoln used a quaint phrase to express his thinking habits: "I don't feel easy 'til I have turned my thoughts all 'round, north, south, east and west."

When you've turned your thoughts "all 'round," your talk should be so conceived and organized that it can be summed up in one or two sentences. You will have divided the main idea into smaller ideas and arranged these in the best logical order to help you put the main idea over. Then, with a provocative, attention-getting "hooker" for an opening and a concise conclusion for your ending, you'll be well on your way.

While preparing his first talk, a client of mine observed, "My wife read it and said, 'George, I never realized what a deep thinker you are!'" He smiled jokingly as he told me, but anyone could have seen he was pleased. Most people underestimate their capacity to think and speak interestingly. If you would begin to put your ideas on paper, you'd soon see what a wealth of experience comes out. Be patient while you're preparing, and you'll be proud of the results.

Jack Glasser, as publicity director for National Distillers, has worked with many top-notch people. He writes of the experiences he has had with "two of the greatest speakers I have ever worked with": W. W. Wachtel, president of Calvert Distillers, and B. C. Ohlandt, executive vice-president of National Distillers.

Both of them began at the bottom in the grocery business, but each of them today earns well over $150,000 a year.

Wachtel, an advertising manager at the age of twenty-six, might still be in that spot, earning probably about $15,000 a year. He was asked to make a speech to salesmen explaining advertising, usually a dull subject for them because there isn't much new that a salesman can be told about. Wachtel was so interesting that the president of Loose-Wiles Biscuit Company asked him to join the firm. More speaking assignments came Wachtel's way, and before you knew it, he was out in the field making speeches to grocer trade associations, where he got a reputation as a crusader for the rights of small businessmen. Soon Wachtel became vice-president in charge of the East. Then he moved on, at double his salary, to become president of Calvert.

The same pattern applied to Ohlandt. He was a salesman for Lipton Tea, covering grocery stores. By speaking up at meetings he attracted attention and soon began to go up the ladder until he became president of Grocery Products Company. From there he went into the liquor industry.

These men never worked together, but both make a fetish of preparing every speech. Their methods are almost identical: First, they have a session with me. We discuss subject, themes, and implications in terms of trade and consumer reactions. We then tell the research people what material to collect. Wachtel and Ohlandt review all this information, make marginal notes, and pass it along to me. I write a first draft. They read this and make changes and notes. Additional drafts follow until we have a speech that could be read verbatim. But here's the switch. Neither would ever think of reading a speech. Each one makes an outline based on the final draft but never memorizes. The outline is a series of phrases—and they use it just to keep them on the track.

Chapter Forty-one

HOW YOUR TALK
COMES TO LIFE

Unless you're giving a "treasurer's report," use facts and figures sparingly—the way lovely women use perfume. Facts are most effective when in the proper frame of reference: compare them with familiar things and space them far apart. The more facts and figures you give your audience, the less important each becomes, and the less they will remember. So always ask yourself: "Is this fact or figure necessary?"

The last time Bob Hope worked his chatter around facts and figures, Columnist Hoffman of the *Hollywood Reporter* was there to quote him:

Today my heart beat 103,389 times, my blood traveled 168,-000,000 miles, I breathed 23,040 times, I inhaled 438 cubic feet of air, I spoke 4,800 words, moved 750 major muscles, and I exercised 7,000,000 brain cells. I'm tired.

As you rehearse your talk, you will want to change and refine it according to "how it listens." That's how your talk comes to life.

Just as important as a "fast-sprint" finish are your opening lines. Your first remark sets the attitude and altitude of your entire talk; be sure to give it extra-special treatment.

Winston Churchill, who always memorizes his speeches and then rehearses before a mirror to study his gestures, records all his talks in advance to check for clarity, voice quality and general structure. A recording or dictating machine will be invaluable during your public-speaking improvement sessions. With its help you'll be able to hear yourself as others hear you. You'll find, too, that this procedure will help your memory.

Some speakers try to memorize every word of their talks, but most people find so much memorizing too much of a strain. Besides, it takes time to memorize a talk properly. Some TV announcers and commentators, who must be letter-perfect and use the exact words, find it difficult to memorize even a one-minute commercial. They depend on the teleprompter, a machine unseen by the audience that electrically moves large type around a roller.

Some time ago, when a prominent government official was speaking on television, an incident in the studio caused considerable embarrassment. Suddenly the prompting machine broke down, and there the speaker was, stranded in the middle of a "what I ... er. ..." No doubt a very busy man, he was not well enough prepared to continue the thought and, lacking the next few words, he had to stop when the machine stopped.

Instead of trying to memorize their talks word for word, I suggest to my clients that they have firmly in mind the main ideas in each paragraph. Only the most skilled speaker can deliver a word-for-word talk so expertly that his audience never knows he has done it that way.

A well-rehearsed talk will still contain many of the original phrases of the written speech, but it's the ideas and your personal speaking techniques that ensure the success of your speech. Speaking from notes gives you the freedom to make contact with your audience—and that's the only way a speaker can put his talk across.

When speakers leave their written-out speech at home and attempt to talk from notes, they may be unnerved by the silence that surrounds them while they're searching for the right word. For an alert speaker who is well prepared, these silent pauses are a plus value. While waiting for him to find the word, the audience themselves are trying to anticipate what the word will be. This participation keeps the audience in suspense and holds their attention.

A little experience proves to the prepared speaker that he can relax and trust his memory—the right word will come. The more we speak, the more we exercise our memory.

I understand that Winston Churchill exercises his memory by learning song lyrics. He knows by heart the words of every musical comedy song hit of the past twenty years.

People usually underrate their memories. Actually, your memory is far better than you think. Even if you claim your memory isn't good, it's probably only rusty. A little sharpening is all it needs. The more a person already knows, the easier it is for him to learn something new. Memory operates by associating the new item with things a person already knows. And the more mental images "on file," the more "hooks" there are for new ideas to be fastened to—and the better the memory.

The way to improve your memory is to help yourself remember. Have a pencil and paper with you all the time, and make notes of anything that you think may be useful. The wisdom in the Chinese saying "Faintest ink better than best memory" has proved its usefulness over the centuries.

It is generally recognized that reading a talk reduces its effectiveness. A great deal of smooth technique and experience are required to read a speech and make it sound natural and unstilted. One of the "pros" who is able to sound spontaneous while delivering a prepared speech is toastmaster George Jessel. In his book *This Way Miss*, he writes:

Since I began speaking at functions at the White House, I have put every word of my speeches on paper, because the first time I spoke at a function in Washington, which was arranged for me by the New York columnist Leonard Lyons (he had told FDR that I would make him laugh), I came to the Capitol and was asked to send my speech in so that it might be read to be sure that it would offend no one. Up to that time I had never put a speech entirely on paper; sometimes I used only a few notes and sometimes none at all. Since then, because of making four or five speeches a week on various subjects, I prepare them well in advance and write every line, and even some gags that sound completely impromptu. Of course my speeches do not sound like I am reading them, because it has been my business all my life not to make them sound so.

George Jessel has experimented and solved his special speaking problems in his own way. But remember that even the professional speaker must start with the same techniques that everybody else uses.

Suppose you have written out your talk and studied it. It is very important for you to retain all the points in your talk, but you want to condense it. Let's say you have ten pages of script and you want to talk from ten "sentence reminders" that will serve as the notes for your talk.

For smooth progress try a technique I have developed in directing and coaching speakers, announcers and performers for radio and television. This method of processing and rehearsing written-out talks is the best method for retaining all the values of the script while permitting the delivery to be natural and spontaneous.

Cover every third paragraph of every page of your written talk with a blank strip of paper (attach it with a staple or piece of cellophane tape to the side margins). Sum up each of the blanked-out paragraphs in one sentence and write the "sentence reminders" on the proper strips. Now rehearse your talk aloud. When you come to each of the substitute sentences, ad lib the information in the paragraph that it covers. In other words, expand the sentence and give about as much time as you would if you were reading the paragraph itself. As you get into the swing, while first covering every third paragraph, then two out of three, and finally, all paragraphs—you will have a substitute sentence for every paragraph in the entire script of your talk.

Follow through by summing up the substitute sentences on each page into "one-page sentences"—one for each page. If your speech is made up of ten pages, you should finish up with ten sentences. These sentences, when typed on one—or ten—small cards—will be useful as a guide during your talk. Naturally, as you practice you will flip over the masking paper if you need to refer to the script.

In rehearsing your talk as many times as necessary, you will find that your last run-through is very different from the first. It will be more appealing—more interesting. When you finally deliver this talk, you can be certain that your public speaking will show a greater poise and confidence than you ever thought possible.

As you rehearse your speeches, learn to time yourself with a stop watch or clock. Find out how long it takes you to develop each of the various ideas. Also find out in advance the time allowed for your talk. Anticipate possible changes. If you're scheduled to talk for twenty minutes, and you're asked just before you begin to cut the time in half, be ready to make adjustments (a tentative cut—or spread). If you have a choice, make it—like the old woman's dance—short and sweet. Remember also that digressions are often the most interesting part of a talk and receive the most rewarding reactions from an audience. Figure on these in your timing.

Learn to apply the radio-TV technique of "backtiming." Know beforehand how long your closing remarks will take and, in addition, the time of the unit that precedes this closing. Then, even if you've used up your time allotment, you will still be able to cut down the next-to-the-last unit and finish on time. The ability to make last-minute adjustments while speaking will give you assurance and poise and make speaking in public a pleasure.

Arrange to try out your talk on a live audience (one or more friends, assistants, secretary), if possible. Choose people who are for you—but who will be objective. Note their reactions—you'll find these useful when you consider possible changes. The more you rehearse, the more you will refine and clarify what you say and how you say it.

Don't try to "cement" your talk into your memory. Allowing yourself freedom to make changes will add color, clarity and action to your talk—and give it that impromptu quality that sustains interest.

Chapter Forty-two

GO INTO ACTION

When Demosthenes, perhaps the greatest orator of all time, was asked what three things made the perfect orator, he answered: "Action! Action! Action!" Commenting on this, Joseph Roux remarked:

...Action! What does this signify? Did he mean gesture? Voice? Attitude? Bearing? Delivery? Movement of idea? The vivacity of images? ... Yes. All this at once.

The "video" part of your talk—gestures and pantomime—adds power to your presentation. Platform movements—using your hands, turning your head, a facial expression—all these give emphasis to your words, hold attention, and dramatize the meaning of your talk.

Practice your talk before a full-length mirror. Make your hand and arm movements broad enough for everyone to see. Use different gestures to punctuate different meanings. Give your face a lift with a few basic expressions—a warm smile, for instance. Going through the same motions again and again has a dulling and monotonous effect. For example, most people find it distracting for a speaker to repeatedly remove and replace his glasses. Use gestures that will fit the flow of your words. And watch your timing; your gesture should precede or be made simultaneously with the emphasized words.

Most speakers are too conservative with gestures. Because they feel awkward or are unfamiliar with the kinds of gestures that best emphasize different ideas, they shy away from gestures altogether. "Shucks," a man will say, "I don't want to be an actor." But you don't have to be an actor to use gestures effectively. A few gestures can go a long way to help you put your points across.

First, limber yourself up with some broad gestures. Say "north" and try to "touch" the ceiling. Next say "south" and reach all the way down to the floor. Say "east" and fling out your right arm to the right. And as you say "west," fling your other arm to the left.

It's surprising how definite and broad a speaker's gestures must be to be understood by a large number of people. Have you ever noticed how broad an umpire makes his gestures for "out" and "safe"? Try a few gestures right now; pantomime the meaning of these phrases:

Come closer—come on, everybody—come up closer.

We don't want that. We never wanted it—and we never will.

Now speak these phrases while you make the appropriate gestures:

All of you—every single one of you sitting here tonight—belongs here with us.

Gentlemen, we must whip this thing and we've got to do it NOW!

Let us have justice in this matter. Let us be fair. Let us weigh each side very carefully.

One man was big and strong and husky. The other was thin and small.

Oh, it was hot all right. It was so hot we nearly passed out.

A loudspeaker system can inhibit gestures because it forces the speaker to stand close to the microphone. However, after a little experimenting in an empty auditorium, you should be able to modify your gestures enough to be able to stay within "mike" range. The top of the microphone should never come above the chin—the audience wants to see your face.

When you speak without a microphone, try stepping away from the speaker's stand. Come forward toward your audience when you're making an important point. Give the feeling you're taking everyone present into your confidence. The longer you remain in one position, the less emotional release your audience will experience—and the less attention you will retain. Although I am certainly not recommending wild waving of arms, purposeless gestures or moving about without rhyme or reason, when I see a "motionless" speaker I sometimes think almost any movement is better than none.

Action helps to put over your words. Free yourself for action, and learn to gesture for the vitality of successful speaking.

Chapter Forty-three

KEEPING YOUR
AUDIENCE INTERESTED

Start strong! Wham! "Give 'em blood in the eye!" is what the late Herbert Bayard Swope told his reporters—and when they hit hard circulation increased.

Did you know that our normal attention span lasts only from five to eight seconds? Like the pendulum of a clock—attention swings first toward the speaker and then away. What, then, must a good speaker do to keep reviving attention?

Your first thirty seconds are vital. If you can make them sit up at the beginning, you've got a good start on holding audience interest to the end.

Do you know Sam Goldwyn's secret of making great pictures? "I want a film that begins with an earthquake and works up to a climax!"

Ask questions! Consult with your audience—take them along with you. Try this, for example: "Do you know that this has been happening all along? How can we explain that?" (pause) "I'll tell you how," you say....

Hit 'em where they live! Is your audience made up of men? Women? Or is it a mixed group? What is the age

range? Younger people "love" adventure, romance. A more
mature audience wants practical, bread-and-butter talk. Do
most of the listeners have children? Is there something
special about the community—good vacation spot, historic
landmark?

When Will Rogers came to a new town, he would visit
the local newspaper office or talk to someone at the town's
chamber of commerce. When it was time for his speech, he
always added the personal touch that people love—he
would name names and pinpoint community interest and
events. Sometimes he'd good-naturedly chide a town official
—and his audience would howl with glee.

Show your enthusiasm and sincerity! If you want people to pay attention to you, look directly at them—not over
or through them, but directly at them. Warming up to
them will help overcome feelings of self-consciousness on
your part; it also helps your audience to be more comfortable. Show your zest and enthusiasm—they'll respond to
you. Establish a friendly relationship with your audience.

A speaker's sincerity can often make up for shortcomings
in his technique. As former President Harry S. Truman has
said, "Sincerity, honesty and a direct manner are more important than special talent or personal polish in speaking."

Announcer Byron Carlson, a client who made his reputation as television spokesman for Eastman Kodak and Olin-
Mathieson, refers to what he calls the three "S's" essential
to the delivery of TV and radio commercials: "Simplicity,
sincerity, sympathy." He says, "Experience has taught me
to speak only about products I can sell sincerely."

Make it unpredictable! Why do you watch a football
game? Because it has suspense—it's unpredictable. How
does a halfback carry the ball? He zigzags, runs, twists and

turns. If the other team knew where he intended to go, he couldn't get very far.

You can add a touch of suspense to your speaking by varying your voice, tempo and body position. That's what Robert Montgomery helped President Dwight D. Eisenhower learn how to do. One of the speaking techniques the President adopted was to gesture when he made transitions in thought. Try making some transitions yourself—on this page—between each paragraph and the one following.

Pause to give importance! Good talk needs to be framed in silence—the pause. Words and ideas need time to sink in. What would you think of a speaker who sounded like this: "Gentlemen: We ... uh ... are ... er ... faced ... er ... with a ... uh ... crisis ... er ... the likes ... uh ... er ... of which ... er ... I have ... never ... uh ... seen before!" Many speakers who fill needed pauses with "static" don't realize how much it interferes with meaning and attention.

On the other hand, a misplaced pause can chop up even the best ideas into a jig-saw puzzle. Make use of the pause —but only after a unit of thought. At a banquet the other night one speaker had a pause pattern like this: "I am happy ... to ... be here ... tonight ... on this ... the ... hundredth ... anniversary ... of our ... organization." This "when-will-he-drop-the-other-shoe?" tempo makes for a boring talk and loses audience attention. Words are links which become a chain of thought only when they are joined together in phrases.

Change the rhythm, pace and pitch! Use variations in rhythm and timing to make your talk expressive and interesting. Figure out and mark the parts that get the most stress—the rest of the talk should go more quickly. Then change the pace of your phrases and vary the pitch of your voice, according to the meaning and feeling.

One night when Robert Benchley was reviewing plays, he found himself completely bored at a performance that went on and on. The play was amateurishly written in a so-called native dialect. After the ingénue lead delivered the line, "Me Nubi. Me good girl. Me stay," Benchley sighed, stood up, and mumbled, "Me Bobby. Me bad boy. Me go!"

Use the words that ring a bell! Use words that create sounds and pictures—impressions that will make people feel and relive their own experiences and sensations. For instance, "We passed the bakery and caught a delicious whiff of freshly baked bread" will do more for your audience than, "We passed the bakery and saw the bread."

Mark Twain once made a remark I value so highly that I've always kept it on my desk: "The difference between the right word and the almost-right word is the difference between lightning and the lightning bug."

As you plan your talk, try to find the words and values that will help the audience hear, feel, "see" and understand your message. We don't all have to be known as deep thinkers, but nobody wants to be known for a "water bug" mind—the kind that skims the top without going underneath the surface.

For top interest—"show them how"! A motherly type of woman I know commented with some pride recently: "My talks are going over because they're like my layer cakes. Just as my cakes have a delicious filling between each layer, so my talks are flavored with illustrations and stories. And," she laughingly added, "that makes my audience real sweet."

Sports Illustrated magazine writer-editor Mort Sharnik has probably solved many a problem with an illustration.

He tells of one: A friend, a young father whose wife had been delayed and wasn't home yet, nervously phoned the Sharniks' and said he didn't have the faintest idea of how to diaper the baby. Mort's wife explained how to the new father but couldn't make him understand. She drew a diagram for Mort and put him on the phone. Mort then translated directions to the new papa that he got—pronto. "Spread the diaper out like a baseball diamond. Make out you're at bat. Fold second base over home plate. Then put baby on the pitcher's mound. Now, pin first, third and home all together."

The best illustration is a demonstration. During your talk, show them how. Make them get the sensation—in word, gesture and expression—if you possibly can.

One of my clients became so upset about his personal problems that he couldn't go on with his work. And he couldn't understand why I couldn't help him as long as his worries weighed him down. "Why," he asked, "do you say no one can help me but myself?"

"Well, let me see," I said, "maybe I can show you what I mean. Would you like to try an experiment?"

When he said, "Fine, let's try it," I instructed him as follows:

"Stand up and I'll try my best to lift you—but you resist." I took a firm grip around his waist and even though I used all my strength I couldn't budge his 143 pounds.

Then I said, "Now on the second try, don't resist. Cooperate by relaxing." This time—with his cooperation—I lifted him easily and quickly.

As we went through this demonstration he was able to "see"—to experience—the idea I had tried earlier to explain in words: Until he cooperated, no one could help him.

A client whose hobby is fishing has a reminder on his desk: "For audience bait—demonstrate." One I've had on my desk reads: "All talk and no illustration makes Jack a dull boy."

Make them laugh and they'll love you! Humor—the right kind at the right time—helps build audience good will and interest. By this, I don't mean that you always have to tell a joke. Part of the adventure and fun of speaking is to find anecdotes that fit. Humor that is in bad taste or out of place is as flat as yesterday's champagne. Speaking with a twinkle in your eye creates an atmosphere of humor— even when you're not going to tell a story.

There are times when a speaker wants to create a feeling of amusement, to call forth a warm response from his audience. A client of mine tells of his success at creating such an atmosphere during a speech to business executives. He needed to introduce the idea of "imagination" before making his point. Mentioning a prominent European who was kidding his American friend about Americans having no imagination, he continued with, "Americans have no imagination? Has he ever heard the average American tell how much better he could run the business than his boss?"

Humor spreads good fellowship all around—it creates a mint-flavored exhilaration that relaxes and "lifts" your audience. Every good speaker knows that an audience that is laughing is with him. An audience that's smiling and laughing is with you—is paying attention—and that means you are making your mark in public speaking.

Chapter Forty-four

LET THEM HEAR YOU!

"Suddenly the mike went dead—and I almost died of embarrassment. Nobody could hear me!" I hope you never have such an experience.

A well-trained speaker anticipates mechanical breakdown—simply because it can happen. However, you should always be able to project your voice so that everyone can hear you without a loudspeaker—except in a large auditorium with very poor acoustics. Speaking without a microphone set-up offers two important advantages: better audience contact and freedom from distortions heard in many loudspeaker systems.

If you deliver a talk that the audience can't hear, why talk? If the audience can't hear you very well—barely hears a phrase now and then—the results are less than zero. Giving a talk that the audience can't hear reminds me of the eccentric millionaire who built two swimming pools: one *with* water and one *without* water—for those who couldn't swim!

There are no two ways about it—a speaker must make himself heard and clearly understood! By observing your audience you can learn to judge distance and volume, the

guides you need in controlling your voice power. If necessary and desirable, you can ask the people in the rear row
to raise their hands if they can't hear you. But keep watching your audience for clues. Usually they show discomfort
by "listening hard," squinting their eyes, coughing or other
noises. When an audience is comfortable, you'll see them
leaning back, relaxing and reacting favorably to what you
say.

At a recent function I heard a prominent official ha-
ranguing his audience in a loud voice with an oratorical
delivery. Too bad he couldn't hear his ear-splitting voice
as it came over the loudspeakers. The audience did, though
—and reacted with a wave of restless coughing, shuffling
and even whispered complaints. The speaker continued,
blissfully unaware of the obvious signs to adjust his voice.

To project your voice successfully you must enunciate
clearly. When I give a talk on public-speaking techniques,
I demonstrate the advantages of clear articulation in voice
projection. First I speak in a very loud voice while using
careless articulation. People are amazed to find that even
loud speaking can be completely unintelligible. Then I
speak in a voice so soft it's actually a loud whisper, but I
enunciate clearly. This time everyone understands every
word. It is immediately obvious to all that poor enunciation and lack of clarity go hand in hand.

Recently, a group of beauties (including the current
"Miss Rheingold"), to be featured on a national television program, were sent to me for help in improving
their dramatic delivery and voice projection. Within four
hours they were able to project their voices—without loudspeakers—in a theater that seats 500 people. The most
vital technique they put to use was to articulate with
energy. It's the clarity of your sounds in speaking that gives
your voice the carrying power for distance.

When you think you have brought your voice power up

to a good projection level, experiment in an empty auditorium to test your voice with a friend. Remember, though, that you have to speak louder when people are present—clothes and people absorb sound.

Speaking loud enough for all to hear helps you give contrast and added importance to your ideas and words. It is voice power that gives you confidence and persuasive appeal.

Chapter Forty-five

OTHERS SPEAK
WITHOUT TENSION—
WHY NOT YOU?

"The human brain is a wonderful thing. It starts working the moment you are born, and never stops until you stand up to speak in public." So quipped toastmaster George Jessel.

Many people who find public speaking a nerve-wracking experience may very well remark, "I wish I could laugh, too—but it hurts too much." They are so right. Anyone who's tense while talking in public can't laugh it off very easily. As a swimmer must be alert to the force of ocean waves, so the speaker must be aware of the power of his tensions.

Either by accident or plan some public speakers have found a workable method to reduce their tensions. Others haven't made out so well. Some have decided they are going to speak, no matter what the pain or sacrifice—like the Marines taking a beachhead. Others have been so stunned by their first experiences in public speaking that they feel they couldn't face an audience again.

Two attempts to gain calmness are widely used, but neither ever turns the trick. First, there's the "fortifying" approach: "Ah, c'mon, buddy. Lemme pour you another.

That'll do it." Another ineffective method is the "Oh, forget it; don't even think about it" routine, long since punched full of holes by psychologists. For instance, if someone tells you, "*Forget* the *elephant*—don't even think about it!" what will you do? Try *not* to think of an *elephant*, of course. Just try it! See what I mean? You can think of nothing else *but* an *elephant*.

Many people have built up so much fear of speaking in public that their tensions get out of hand. Lack of information or outmoded ideas frequently cause them to misinterpret their nervous reactions. Many people over-react to tension by becoming panicky. Some people over-estimate the importance of saying a few words in public and suffer from tensions because they are oversensitive, and perhaps a bit too self-conscious. They over-react to their tensions instead of making peace with their nervous systems and calmly accepting a certain amount of discomfort.

Many experienced speakers and performers have succeeded in mastering their tensions, but they are never completely at ease—and don't want to be. They believe that a "keyed-up" feeling helps them "put it over," and they are right. Since these people know they have something to contribute, they accept their tensions and follow through effectively. They are genuine, sincere and take their responsibilities seriously. Edward R. Murrow, for example, is still gnawed by nerves before and during his broadcasts. Even in perfectly air-conditioned studios I've watched him drip perspiration because of tension.

On his first show Ed Sullivan was so paralyzed with tension that he received many letters from viewers congratulating him on his triumph over facial paralysis, a twisted back and other illnesses he had never had. Experience and success have made him feel a thousand times more at ease, but even now he still feels some tension.

An executive who was making good progress in improving his speaking technique asked me, "Will I ever be completely at ease when I speak?" My answer was, "Maybe you won't want to be." I assured him that with more speaking experience his confidence would increase, and that he would feel more at ease. Then I explained how his "keyed-up" sensations contributed to his effectiveness.

A businessman wanted to know if a calming method used by a friend would also help him. His friend's gimmick: "I just look at the faces out front and I think they're a bunch of cabbages." "Well, how would you like it," I asked him, "if a speaker thought of you as a cabbage?"

Many years ago Winston Churchill, then a young member of Parliament, arrived for his first talk in the company of Lord Salisbury, a veteran statesman. Lord Salisbury, noticing Churchill's tension, turned and said, "If you're feeling nervous, Winston my boy, do what I do. When I rise to speak I look around at the audience and say to myself, 'What a lot of silly fools.' Then I feel much better." An amusing approach, perhaps, but not recommended to anyone who honestly wishes to reduce nervous tension. I hardly believe Mr. Churchill used it. Isn't it antagonistic and self-defeating to think of your audience as "a lot of silly fools"?

A successful speaker is one who likes to speak—one who likes and respects his listeners. He comes close to what George Jessel said about Jack Benny: "... you can tell by what he says that he likes everybody. I never heard him say an unkind word in private or before the public."

An attorney who learned to control his tensions and now delivers about one talk a week still remembers how intensely nervous he used to feel. He recalled my telling him this anecdote from Carl Sandburg's *Abraham Lincoln: The War Years*, which helped him look at himself less seriously:

After an evening at the White House a friend asked Lincoln, "How does it feel to be President of the United States?" He replied: "You've heard about the man who was tarred and feathered and ridden out of town on a rail? A man in the crowd asked him how he liked it and his reply was that if it wasn't for the honor of the thing, he would rather walk."

Speaking in public is an honor as well as a responsibility. No doubt you respect that responsibility. You feel that your audience deserves your best. If you've been discouraged by your tensions, remember this: others have mastered their tensions—by facing the facts, making peace with their nervous system, and reducing physical tension. You can also benefit from following these same techniques—and help yourself gain a new confidence while speaking in public.

Chapter Forty-six

CONQUER YOUR FEARS
BY FACING THE FACTS

A TV personality whose performances had begun to draw low audience ratings confided to me: "I was a wise guy who couldn't face the facts! I fought everybody on my staff. I was even fool enough to try to 'fight' the audience! Well, I found out there's only one way to fight an audience— with your hat—grab it and run!" This performer learned the hard way. He's since made a comeback—and his new attitude and performances have been very well received.

If you're nervous when you speak in public, don't just try to brush your nervousness aside. And don't attempt to force a false front by smiling with quivering lips. People who are able to admit openly their weaknesses worry less and feel less tension. No less a person than Albert Einstein freely admitted his weaknesses and mistakes. And don't feel you have to apologize for your weaknesses. Other people appreciate sincerity and humility and will often understand.

Nervous tension is an emotional reaction that snowballs when we are under stress, especially when we feel helpless and don't know what to do. It reaches an importance all out of proportion, largely because we are afraid of it.

I recently listened to one man tell of his tension. As his name is announced and he rises to speak, his mouth goes dry, his knees feel weak and his heart palpitates. "A wave of tension sweeps over me," he reports, "and I get tied up in sailor's knots." As his fears mount he perspires, he trembles. As a result, his fears increase—tension and nervousness mount even higher. The tension circle is set in motion—the snowball snowballs. He is afraid because he is nervous—nervous because he's fearful.

It is normal to be afraid of the unknown. As we begin to understand what is happening and why, it's as if the lights in a strange, dark room full of disturbing shadows had just been turned on. The room lights up, the shadows disappear, the room is no longer strange and dark. It's the same when we face unpleasant facts—in this case, the facts about nervous tension.

During the time a person is under tension, his nervous system—normally so beautifully organized—could be said to be "over-organized." Once the nervous system is alerted by fear, the body prepares for "emergency action": "All glands at battle stations!" The demand for more oxygen speeds up breathing, the need for faster circulation quickens the heartbeat, and the call for more energy is met by increased supplies of blood sugar and adrenalin. When a person begins to understand and calmly accept such physiological reactions, he can make this ready "super-energy" serve a positive purpose. Facing the facts enables him to use this super-energy in such a way as to relieve his fears and increase his chances of success.

A prominent clubwoman first had to overcome a childhood of "little praise and lots of disapproval" before she was able to master her tensions and make progress with her speaking techniques. Her experience is similar to that of many people who are blocked by tensions in speaking.

In describing one childhood incident that had touched

off her fears later in life, she said that when she was about three she had been bitten by a dog. When I asked if she had always been afraid of dogs after that, she replied, "I was nervous with dogs for a while—but soon I learned how to make friends with them. I have two adorable cocker spaniels now, and I don't know what I'd do without them."

"In other words," I continued, "you're not afraid anymore that dogs will bite you. You've learned how to make adjustments—just as you are now learning how to overcome tension while speaking. You have learned how to face the facts!"

Chapter Forty-seven

MAKE PEACE WITH
YOUR NERVOUS SYSTEM

Sometimes I go sailing with a family of friends who own two pedigreed Irish setters. On one especially hot July day we thought we'd cool off by taking a swim. The small daughter was the first to dive in, and the rest of us followed.

We'd hardly got wet when the dogs, not kept on leash, suddenly leaped into the water. Having been on no "swimming parties" before, they apparently were of the opinion that their eight-year-old mistress needed to be saved. Once in the water, they wildly pawed and pushed her small body under water, almost drowning her and themselves in their effort to "save" her. We pulled the little girl up on the boat and finally managed to fish the panicky dogs out of the water, dry them and tie them up. The little girl coughed up some water and her parents, touched by the setters' loving concern for their small daughter, managed to laugh off an experience that could have been serious.

This incident is a simplified analogy of the way our sympathetic nervous system operates, how it wildly tries to take over—to "save us" when we become apprehensive. And —like the dogs—our nervous system, operating on "primitive standard time," over-reacts. As philosopher-scientist

Bertrand Russell explained: "Our instinctive emotions are those that we have inherited from a much more dangerous world, and contain, therefore, a larger proportion of fear than they should."

Now what actually happens to your body when you become tense and nervous? Your muscles are tense, in preparation for fight or escape; but there's no real reason for you to do either. All you want to do is stay where you are.

Your heart is pumping faster and your breathing tempo has increased—your body's response to excitement or crisis. Now, is there a crisis? Only if you think so. If you will recognize your nervous system as "the good guy" and not regard it as a "villain," you will reduce the number and intensity of reactions which interfere with effective speaking.

When your heart begins to beat faster, say to yourself: "Okay, dear heart. Thanks for the help. But we don't need all that pumping. Slow down—we'll be okay." As your breathing becomes more rapid, think: "I'm breathing faster to get rid of the carbon dioxide and to get more oxygen."

Breathe deeply and rhythmically to help the natural process, to calm yourself and feel more relaxed. A drink of water will make you feel more comfortable. Starting your talk and continuing with it will use that ready energy, restore your self-esteem and diminish the tensions.

As you become able to anticipate your reactions, you will find that you can make peace with your nervous system by putting the new routine into operation. As you gain practice in quickly and "automatically" soothing your alerted nerves, you'll find that your tensions will subside. Eventually, there will come a day when you will be certain of controlling your tension while speaking. That's when you'll be free to speak with purpose and poise.

Chapter Forty-eight

RAPIDLY RELAXING
PHYSICAL TENSIONS

People say: "Every time I have to speak, my muscles tighten up. Is there something I can do that will help me relax?"

For rapid relaxation, try these suggestions that my clients have found to be very practical. Simply tense your muscles —stretch out—hold it for a moment—then release and relax. This exercise can be done while you're sitting or standing. Just before going on, while you're backstage, is a good time to stretch out and relax. There's no need to be self-conscious because this exercise can be done in a way that no one will notice.

To break that out-of-breath feeling, yawn a few times. Since yawning causes the body to relax, forcing a few yawns is an excellent start. To gain calmness, breathe slowly, deeply and rhythmically. Once on the platform, but before you begin to speak, pause as the audience quiets down, and continue breathing slowly and evenly.

Another way to help yourself relax is to release muscle tension by moving around. Since you can't run around the stage waving wildly (an ideal way if we could use it to release muscle tensions), you must create the oppor-

257

tunities in a socially acceptable way. To public speakers, this means telling a joke or story that calls for action and gestures—broad gestures. Also, if the anecdote you start your talk with is funny and the audience laughs, they will relax and their reaction will make you feel more at home. That's the perfect way to start giving a talk.

You may also wish to try these exercises that are designed to help you relax before you start speaking. Rotate your head slowly and gently—and keep stretching your neck. Open your mouth, let the jaw go limp, close your eyes. Now stretch your head back. Rub the back of the neck and shoulders—a prominent tension area. Warm up your voice by making some open crooning sounds like "Bah . . . bee . . . bo . . . boo." Let the sounds ring out.

With your talk well prepared and rehearsed and the "normal" body tensions relaxed, your greatest confidence will come from the way your audience reacts. The people in your audience—when they are informed and entertained —will show their pleasure, and that is the best vote of confidence any speaker can hope for.

Chapter Forty-nine

HURDLE THE
"SPEAKER'S
STEEPLECHASE"

Once you've learned to jump the "Speaker's Steeplechase,"
not even the most distressing disturbance will upset you
while you're making a speech. Jumping the hurdles will
prepare you for anything that might happen.

Start with a group of ten or more. As each takes turns
delivering a three-to-five-minute talk, the group goes into
action—their object being to challenge the speaker's special weaknesses.

The main purpose is to show the speaker how he can
jump "speakers' hurdles" smoothly—no matter how tricky
they are, and no matter how nervous he is. The speaker's
hurdles are any and all possible distractions, interruptions
and other irritating annoyances.

If it's known that the speaker is disturbed by people walking around the room or by whispering, that's exactly what
the others should do to be most helpful to him. Other
sound effects—usually unintentional—that can unnerve
some speakers are shuffling of feet, coughing, talking and
whispering in the audience, people walking in and out,
sudden laughter.

One member of the "audience" might stop the speaker
to ask a "loaded" question. According to the rules, the

speaker must answer without irritation. A speaker who jumps these "hurdles" successfully proves to himself that he can continue his talk—no matter how rough or irritating the hurdles set up by his audience.

No actual speaking situation could be more nerve-wracking than the "Speaker's Steeplechase." After three such sessions, members of the group usually show a remarkable, relaxed confidence. With their tensions under control because they have made the grade, they take themselves less seriously and feel capable of taking on any speaking experience.

The "Speaker's Steeplechase" can really be a lot of fun. In fact, often the only problem is to keep the laughter from dominating the learning experience. You can do that, though, by letting the laughter come first.

Speaking in public has at times been compared to a plunge into cold water. After the first shock, you catch your breath—and then start swimming. As your body warms up, you begin to feel elated. The shock is gone, but the glow of pleasure lingers on.

If, once the chips are down, you begin to have doubts, set your focus on the rewards that make it all worthwhile, so poignantly illustrated by Adrian Anderson in *Along the Way*:

For two decades the great French artist Renoir suffered pain and misery. Rheumatism wracked his body and distorted his fingers. As he slowly applied his paint to the canvas, beads of perspiration stood on his brow, from intense suffering.

Renoir could not stand but had to be placed in a chair, moved up and down to give him access to various parts of his canvas. Yet he persisted, painting in pain masterpieces of girlhood beauty.

Matisse, his disciple, pleaded one day, "Why torture yourself to do more?"

Gazing at a favorite canvas, Renoir replied, "The pain passes, but the beauty remains."

Chapter Fifty

PUBLIC SPEAKING
IMPROVEMENT SESSIONS

START TALKING

Mary Pickford and Douglas Fairbanks, Sr. used to entertain themselves by playing a little game, which is also a favorite of mine. I call it "Start Talking."

Write out—in one word or a short phrase—a different topic on each of several slips of paper, allowing a few topics for every player. Fold the slips and put them into a hat. Each player in turn digs into the hat, chooses a slip, reads the topic, and immediately "Starts Talking"—and keeps it up for thirty seconds.

Then, when all have spoken, fold the slips, put them back in the hat and start over again. The second time around, everyone talks for one minute—and so on—until each player has made a talk that lasts for three minutes.

Just to give you an idea, some one-word topics that have worked well are: tennis, circus, market, travel. For phrase topics, you could start with: The last time I was in Bermuda, Summer in Colorado, My hobby is . . . , Let me tell you about my grandchildren. . . .

Each speaker should treat his talk as he would if he were making a public speech. Have an opening statement, follow with a short talk, and make a concluding remark. If you wish, arrange for the group to give demerits for mannerisms and apologies ("I don't know what to say" or "Gosh") or anything else that reduces poise. Say the first words that come to mind for best results. Learn to overlook "fluffs" and keep going. You can fix it next time around.

Supposing your topic is tennis, you could open your talk with: "Tennis can be a lot of fun if you play the game well." You could go on to explain that you don't get a chance to play much these days. Your closing remark? "Maybe next summer I can really brush up on the game and have some fun." Even if you draw a commonplace topic, your talk can be as straightforward as the lines above or as sophisticated as Salvador Dali.

Have someone watch the second hand on a clock or a stopwatch. Stop when he says, "Time's up." Have the timer give signals to the speaker—for instance, ten fingers for ten seconds to go.

At first you may find your "motor slow in starting," but be patient—after a try or two, you'll warm up and really get into the swing. And keep at it. Before you know it, you will become really skilled at thinking and speaking on your feet.

After making about 150 three-minute speeches, a former client reported on his experience with "Start Talking": "It's the best thing that ever happened to me! I've parlayed those three minutes into a speaker's award at my club."

EXPLAIN THE PROVERBS

The French have a saying: "Judge a man by his favorite proverbs." Buy, borrow or beg a book of quotations or proverbs, and use them to make your talking more interesting and colorful. Two or more people can play. Open the book at random, and read the first proverb that catches your eye. Then explain what it means to you. Give other examples—what it reminds you of. Try to be informative and amusing. The ability to form ideas on the spur of the moment will add excellent experience to your public speaking "know-how."

And playing games like those suggested will increase your ability to keep others interested.

TALKING TO CHILDREN

If you want to appreciate the finer points in public speaking, nothing is more rewarding than talking to children. It's an excellent way for you to develop simplicity, humility and directness.

Children naturally react freely—and quickly show their feelings. The person most successful in holding their attention is the one who makes good use of action stories, picture words and gestures.

We can learn a great deal about the demands of speaking to the public from talking with children. They may sometimes try your patience—but so can an adult audience. If you can say and do things that will keep the children interested, they won't take their eyes off you. And the audience of a good speaker will react in the very same way. Try holding the interest of children while you explain something. Be alert to their reactions. Help them explain something to you.

When Ireene Wicker, the well-known "Singing Lady," tells a story to children, her presentation is so effective that she seems to be transformed before your very eyes. Her childlike quality gives you a feeling of simplicity. Alertness and vitality, so clearly evident in Miss Wicker's delivery of her lines, are qualities every public speaker should strive for.

REPORTING THE NEWS

After each person chooses a news story from a newspaper or magazine, all take turns in first reading aloud and then in following—immediately—with a brief, ad lib resume. This resume may be given from previously prepared notes, which should include exact quotes from the story.

When everyone has delivered his news report and resume once, repeat the routine to give each a chance to improve his technique. Searching for the right words or phrases provides good opportunity for learning how to keep calm and well organized during the ad lib portion. "Reporting the News" can help anyone to maintain poise and learn to think and talk with little preparation. The routine, of course, can be applied to any and all types of material.

AND LAST BUT NOT LEAST

Walter Winchell tells a story that makes a point for all of us to ponder:

John Barrymore once consoled a young actress who was in tears over the critics' reviews. "It's easy for you to talk," sighed the novice. "The critics' raves made you a star." "Yes, I know," said Barrymore, "and their bad notices made me an actor!"

Barrymore recognized the refining influence of criticism. As much as he appreciated applause, he learned to "grow on his bad notices." As you learn to speak in public, you will certainly improve by observing yourself. But do not underestimate your good fortune when valued acquaintances—or anyone in the audience—gives you a tip that helps you become the speaker you want to be.

Some years ago James A. Farley, in telling me about his method of speaking successfully, said:

You will finish some talks feeling not very satisfied with the way things worked out. You may wish you had said or done something different. The best way to get over a talk that has gone sour is to arrange for the next one as soon as you can.

Even if your first few tries aren't very smooth, just keep talking. Before you know it, you may find yourself too popular a speaker to stop.

Robert Benchley used to talk about the way he became a popular writer. He summed up his career in these words:

It took me fifteen years to discover I had no talent for writing. But I couldn't give it up because by that time I was too famous.

ABOUT THE AUTHOR

Stephen S. Price, lecturer, writer, and former speech adviser and director at Columbia Broadcasting System, has coached many famous people in the entertainment, political, and business fields. In fact, his entire professional career has been dedicated to the spoken word. He has worked as actor, director, and stage manager for touring stock companies; production aide in Broadway plays; director and coach in summer stock, radio announcer and newscaster. During the war he became a producer for the Office of War Information and also lectured to Air Force pilots on communications. Later he became Chief of Program Production and was on the Program Planning Board for Radio Free Europe. During his busy career Mr. Price has had time to earn his master's degree in Speech, Psychology, and Communications at Teachers College, Columbia University. Mr. Price has always been interested in helping public speakers, actors, and broadcasters improve their delivery and speak more effectively; he now has his own speech-consultant studio and most of his time in recent years has been devoted to individual coaching, lecturing, and writing. In addition to speaking before groups in various parts of the country he has lectured at Columbia University, New York University, and Hunter College. His articles on speech have appeared in *The Reader's Digest, The American Weekly,* and other magazines.